[Plot Twist]

God enters
stage left

TIM DAY

the meeting
house
a church for people who aren't into church

ISBN-13: 978-1-61291-617-0

Cover design by Joss Monzon
Cover image by Shutterstock

Some of the anecdotal illustrations in this book are true to life and are included with the permission of the persons involved. All other illustrations are composites of real situations, and any resemblance to people living or dead is coincidental.

Unless otherwise identified, all Scripture quotations in this publication are taken from the *Holy Bible, New International Version*® (NIV®). Copyright © 1973, 1978, 1984, 2011 by Biblica, Inc.® Used by permission of Zondervan. All rights reserved worldwide. www.zondervan.com. The "NIV" and "New International Version" are trademarks registered in the United States Patent and Trademark Office by Biblica, Inc.® Other versions used include: the Holy Bible, New Living Translation (NLT®), copyright © 1996, 2004, 2007 by Tyndale House Foundation, used by permission of Tyndale House Publishers Inc., Carol Stream, IL 60188, all rights reserved; the Common English Bible (CEB), copyright © 2011 by Common English Bible; and the NET Bible® copyright ©1996-2006 by Biblical Studies Press, L.L.C., all rights reserved.

Printed in the United States of America

3 4 5 6 7 8 / 18 17 16 15 14 13

Contents

Foreword

IN THE WRONG hands, the Bible can be used to justify almost anything. Cult leaders and violent religious zealots throughout history have succeeded because of one fact: most people do not know how to read the Bible the way it was intended. The story of the Bible, centering on God's love for us and made undeniably clear through Jesus, is the grand context within which every separate verse, command, and story must be understood. Without the big picture, we can easily miss the point of any given story within the larger story. And when we miss the context, we are left vulnerable to the abusive interpretations of anyone with an agenda.

By helping us get to know the whole story, Tim Day wants to help rescue people from those who abuse Scripture. His book is indispensable for believers, inquirers, and skeptics alike. If you take time with this book, it will help you get the most of your time with that other book, the Bible.

Bruxy Cavey
author of *The End of Religion* and
teaching pastor of The Meeting House

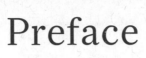

Preface

SOME PEOPLE GROW up feeling as though they are somehow different from others. I grew up feeling very ordinary. My family lived in Sherkston, Ontario, on Sherkston Road, where the "Sherks" live. I do not know if you can get any more small-town than Sherkston.

I am now the senior pastor of a church family in Ontario called The Meeting House. I am married to Liz and have three great kids, Nathan, Rachel, and Joshua. I still feel ordinary in most ways.

I grew up in a Christian family and attended the small church up the road from my home. When I left home, I moved to the United States to obtain an undergraduate degree. I then moved to Toronto to complete my master's degree, and it was there that I started to study the Bible in depth.

I soon discovered that, over my lifetime, I had obtained a lot of facts about the Bible from popular Christian teachers and pastors. I knew a lot of its stories and had gained many insights, but I had never heard much about the Bible's overarching narrative and what it all meant.

Typically, the teachers and pastors I listened to would use specific Bible passages, sometimes taken out of context, to drive home a moral lesson or illustrate why we should trust in God or love others, but they rarely confronted the apparent inconsistencies in the Bible, such as how the warlike God of the Old Testament fits with the peace-loving

God of Jesus in the New Testament. Nor did they confront the atrocities committed in the name of Christianity, such as the Crusades, the Inquisition, or the burning of heretics and so-called witches. They did not address the endless divisions among denominations in relation to the clear teachings of Jesus. Apart from my professors at seminary, I found that most popular Christian teachers and writers generally ignored such issues. That left me wondering how all these issues jived with God's overall story line.

My inner skeptic sent me on a quest to put the pieces together. Over the years, I worked my way through the entire Bible and even wrote my own commentary on it. I also invested years translating entire books of the New Testament. I think this technically makes me a Bible nerd.

In any case, the book you are about to read represents my best attempt to compile a simple, easy-to-read approach to understanding the meaning of the Bible. It is like *The Meaning of the Bible for Dummies*. My hope is that people of all faith positions or skeptical persuasions might find here a simple explanation for what the most popular, most translated, most studied book in history actually means.

There are a number of people I want to thank. First, I want to say a sincere thank you to three scholars who helped me with their insights and encouragement for the book: Dr. Paul Eddy, professor of biblical and theological studies and respected author; Dr. Terry Brensinger, dean of Fresno Pacific Biblical Seminary; and Dr. Ian Scott, associate professor of New Testament studies. Their support and input in the final editing of the book were invaluable to me. Second, I am deeply appreciative of the excellent work of my editor Rick Maranta. His partnership in content development and writing style has significantly shaped the final form of the book. Thank you, Rick. Third, I am thankful for my church family at The Meeting House, in particular the creative and editorial contributions from Joss Monzon, Seth Rowden, Nancy Bishay, and Joel Percy. Finally, I am so grateful for my father and mother, John and Barbara, who first told me the biblical story and what it meant. I dedicate this book to them as a small way to say thank you for all of the ways they have invested in me and my family over the years.

I hope you not only enjoy this story but also become captivated by its vision: people who are changed from the inside out as they learn how to live in friendship with God and one another.

1

Meaning

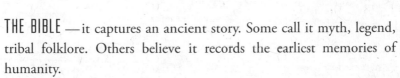

THE BIBLE — it captures an ancient story. Some call it myth, legend, tribal folklore. Others believe it records the earliest memories of humanity.

The people who first told this story, a small nation called Israel, were the nobodies of the ancient world. They were descendants of nomads and slaves living under the oppressive shadow of powerful empires like Egypt and Babylon. They lived on the margins of society with little to offer. No great empire. No powerful army. No amassed wisdom or wealth. They just tried to survive from one generation to the next, sometimes wandering in the hot sun for years.

Although they were the weakest, most vulnerable group of people you could imagine, they had the audacity to claim divine privilege. In a world dominated by belief in multiple gods, they claimed there was only one true God — one who, out of all the powerful nations on earth, had taken special notice of them. The nerve of them.

These people also held a belief that was almost laughable to anyone looking on from the outside. They said a king would come from their humble heritage and would one day establish an eternal kingdom under the domain of the one true God. It sure sounded like this little group of nobodies had delusions of grandeur. All that wandering around in the hot sun must have gotten to them.

Then something completely unexpected happened.

After a few centuries, this small nation once again found itself under an oppressive occupying force: the powerful Roman Empire. Yet from this small, oppressed nation, a movement sprang up that swept the known world. You might call it an underground insurgence, a counter-cultural community, but it came with a kind of fire.

Even though the movement became popular among rich and poor alike, it was severely persecuted. Why? It seems that the religious leaders and the political authority structures of the ruling Roman Empire did not like to share power with anyone, least of all a carpenter's son whom people were calling the King of the Jews and the Son of God. Paranoid dictators can be like that.

As a result, many members of this persecuted group were publicly executed. Many lost their property and personal freedoms. Yet they continued to grow and penetrate every strata of Roman society. Those within the movement believed that they were part of a divine revolution. They believed God's King had come and God was initiating a new kind of kingdom: a transnational network of friendships that would welcome all people, regardless of race, gender, or social caste.

The message they announced was radical, and even offensive to some. They said that all people could live at peace with God without the need for religion, including the temples, rituals, priesthoods, and sacrifices that were an expected part of life for a God-fearing people. Those looking for spiritual connection could find it, not in relentless rituals or strict codes, but in a friendship with God, resulting in the tangible sense of security and hope that love brings. God, as the leader[1] of their lives, would be more like a loving parent than a tyrannical dictator. The message offered freedom, but freedom in community and with responsibility.

The life they shared was enviable. Average people possessed unshakable courage even when faced with severe suffering. They showed radical generosity and compassion to the sick, orphans, widows, and outcasts. Women, slaves, and the poorest of the poor were offered respect and equality within community. Those living in isolation now had family.

Sounds good, yes? Like a dream? I would think so.

As the story unfolded over the centuries, it was written down and collected into a library. This library, which today is contained within a single book we call the Bible, became the primary text for one of the world's largest religions, Christianity. But what if you were told that many people who have stewarded this library and are followers of this religion have, for centuries, acted in ways that contradict the message of the book they claim to follow? Would that seem ironic to you?

What if the story contained in that book invited us into an irreligious friendship with God but we constructed a massive religion based on it instead?

What if the story called us to live lives of peacemaking but we ended up waging war after war in its name?

What if the story challenged us to live simple and sacrificially generous lives but we hoarded our wealth and spent it on lavish living?

What if the story cast a vision for an inclusive unified community but we fostered an atmosphere of constant disagreements and factions throughout history, leading to a legacy of broken relationships and division?

What if the story revealed the key to transforming our lives from the inside out, but we used this story to keep people bound by legalism and insecurity?

This would not be a dream, would it? It sounds more like a nightmare. But that is exactly what happened.

How is this possible, you might ask? How can any group of people read the same book over and over again from generation to generation and just not get it? The answer is simple. Each generation heard the story, but over time it lost its original meaning. People could identify the characters, events, and settings, but they would often miss how the whole drama actually fit together. There are lots of good reasons for this.[2] But the fact remains that even today the meaning of the ancient story found in the Bible has been lost to millions of people around the world. Are you interested in discovering what was lost?

While our narrator steps up to the microphone, feel free to find a comfy chair and grab a cup of coffee. Everyone has a story to tell, even God. It is time to listen again to his story and recapture his heart and vision for humanity. Spoiler alert: plot twists ahead.

2

Perfection

Act One: Genesis 1–2

THE CURTAIN RISES and our story begins.

A mysterious character enters stage left.

He silently takes his place on the center stage of human history.

In the shadows, a darkened audience looks on.

This story contains mystery, drama, romance, and comedy.

But in the end, it is a scandal.

When the curtain closes, the audience will be left in shock.

The first two acts are brief, yet pregnant with meaning. Like the first few minutes of a skillfully crafted mystery, if you miss the opening scenes you will be lost the rest of the way.

The stage is completely empty and black. Our main character speaks a single word in a low quiet whisper and everything we know explodes into existence:

stars and sun,

planets and moons,

water and land,

birds and fish and animals.

The ancients who worship a pantheon of temperamental deities could easily be astounded by this opening account. This god creates with ease. There is no strain or struggle. There is beauty and order.

There is no chaos. This god has ultimate authority, power, and creativity. He[1] is way more powerful than any god they have known. Stunning.

There is something more that strikes those who listen to this ancient tale, something that rocks their religious sensibilities. The opening poetic account of how the world began declares that none of the ancient objects of worship — the sun, moon, stars, rivers, mountains, or living creatures — are actually gods at all. They are just creative expressions of the one true God. This would not do for the Egyptians, who worshipped the sun, moon, earth, sky, wind, and sea.[2] And how would this sound to the Canaanites and Babylonians with their host of nature-based deities? What would the ancient Greeks think about this, with their pantheon of gods and goddesses all corresponding to forces and elements of nature, sun, moon, sky, and wind? Right from the start, this ancient story levels the religious world of its day.[3]

Is it possible that if I continue to listen to this story I will have my religious paradigm rocked?

Once the stage is set, God creates his supporting cast. The audience watches as God gathers up dust, the most frail and worthless stuff available. He breathes his divine Spirit into it, and this dust turns into living, breathing beings. God's Spirit has the power to make dead, worthless things come to life.

Unlike all the other living creatures, God's supporting cast are humans, a man and a woman named Adam and Eve. They carry the actual imprint of God's character and image.[4] The ancients who first heard this account of creation were used to their rulers setting up statues made in their own image in public places to remind their subjects who was in charge. In a sense, the all-powerful God of our story does the same thing, except that he does not make a statue or idol to draw attention to himself. Instead, he creates a man and a woman, who together make up a beautiful relational and spiritual picture (or "image") of God.

And he does not do it to show everyone who is boss.

He does it to create friends.

Then God said, "Let us make human beings in our image, to be like us. They will reign over the fish in the sea, the birds in the sky, the livestock, all the wild animals on the earth, and the small animals that scurry along the ground."

So God created human beings in his own image.
In the image of God he created them;
male and female he created them.

Then God blessed them and said, "Be fruitful and multiply. Fill the earth and govern it. Reign over the fish in the sea, the birds in the sky, and all the animals that scurry along the ground."

Then God said, "Look! I have given you every seed-bearing plant throughout the earth and all the fruit trees for your food. And I have given every green plant as food for all the wild animals, the birds in the sky, and the small animals that scurry along the ground — everything that has life." And that is what happened.

Then God looked over all he had made, and he saw that it was very good!

GENESIS 1:26-31, NLT

God does not stop there. His new friends need a home, so he creates a garden[5] for them to live in, a safe place for them to work and hang out with their Creator. This garden is lush with life because a refreshing river flows through it. He entrusts the whole place to them to nurture, guard, and protect. He makes both Adam and Eve responsible for it, so that they might have purpose for their lives.[6]

It is the perfect setting for God and humanity to live in harmony, partnering together to make an already perfect world even better. It is a world without religion. There are no temples or priests. There are no rituals or rule books. Love is the only guide for their lives as they look forward to an ever-deepening experience of joy and intimacy with

God and with each other. They stand before each other and their Creator completely naked and unashamed.[7]

Fully secure in love, their vulnerability frees them to be truly intimate. When you have nothing to hide, you can share everything. You can be known and loved for who you really are. No facades. No hidden agendas. No secrets. Everything is out on the table. It is only you and it is all of you.

At the deepest level, do I simply want to be loved for who I am?

In a world where love is the only guide, you do not need a long list of rules or a complicated religion. That is why there is only a single boundary for the man and woman to respect. God asks that they not eat from one tree in the garden: the Tree of Knowledge of Good and Evil.

You see, God planted two important trees in the center of the Garden of Eden.

One tree is called the Tree of Life. Eating from it symbolizes life unending and life abundant. God welcomes them to eat freely from this tree. This tree represents a meeting place for their love relationship with God and a way for them to express their commitment to him in a practical way. It offers them the promise that God's life will sustain their lives — spiritually, emotionally, and physically.

The second tree is called the Tree of Knowledge of Good and Evil. Choosing to eat from it results in certain death. This second tree represents self-centered independence.[8] We might call it the "I will decide for myself what is right and wrong" tree. To refrain from eating of this tree would show that Adam and Eve trust God and believe he ultimately knows what is best.

In his wisdom, God knew that for this friendship to work, it had to be based on free choice. Without the ability to leave that relationship, man and woman would have been trapped as prisoners in it. They would have been puppets and playthings rather than true friends and companions. The forbidden tree offers them a way out if they want it. All they have to do is eat of it and they will be making a clear choice between what each tree represents and a strong statement about what they think of their Creator. Yet, the warning not to eat of it could not be stronger. The consequences could not be more clear.

What choice would I make?

Do I want to "decide for myself what is right and wrong"?

And so at the end of Act One, God rests from his creative work and takes time just to be with his friends. In this creation account, we discover that all God wanted was one big happy family — a family that would live in harmony with their heavenly parent in the beautiful world he had created for their enjoyment.

It is a world without religion.

No temple, priest, or rituals.

No social caste or currency.

No police or prison.

No government or armies.

Only love.

Reflection on Perfection

There are moments when I feel like I experience life as it was originally intended.

My first child was born just before midnight. As I held him for the first time, staring into his wide open eyes, it was as if we were both experiencing life for the first time. His tiny frame and vulnerable gaze awakened a love within me I had never known. He was mine and I was his. In that moment, that was all that mattered.

The U.S. Declaration of Independence says, "We hold these truths to be self-evident." However, I would say that not all truths are self-evident. Some truths are counterintuitive. In the early 1600s, for instance, who would have believed that the earth orbited the sun? In those days everyone believed, without a doubt, that the sun moved around the earth, not the other way around. It was obvious. All you had to do was look. But it was not obvious to Galileo, who spent the last part of his life under house arrest for promoting the heretical idea that things were not as they seemed but were in fact the other way around.

Yet there are other truths that we recognize and hold on to that require no defense or explanation. We simply know deep down that they are true. For instance, we all know that parents should love their children, in whatever cultural form that takes.

There is something else common to all people of all times: a yearning for a life of joy and peace without end.

Humanity seems to have this hunch that there is something beyond our physical world, a sense that there is "something bigger" out there. From ancient cave drawings that depict a journey into the afterlife, to the gift- and food-laden tombs of the Pharaohs, to the Mayan temples and ancient places of worship, across the canvas of history we gaze at a picture of people reaching out for more.

The story of creation, the first act of the story of God, helps me make sense of my own heart. It helps me see that my deep desire for a perfect world is not simply a cosmic hoax but actually what I was designed for.

All of the things I long for—love, security, meaning, and a full life that never ends—are the things I was made for. What I hate and fight against—loneliness and failure, hurtful relationships, war, disease, aging, and death itself—are all violent intruders into my existence.

But most shocking to me is what is absent from this opening account of creation.

In God's perfect world there is no religion, no ritual, and no hierarchy. God requires no spiritual ladder of enlightenment or code of ethical behavior to reach him. God's ultimate vision for humanity is completely religion-free. As a heavenly parent, all God ever wanted was a family that understood a simple truth: when love guides every member of the family, the family does not really need rules because love is greater than law.

As a parent, I completely get this. I have three children, Nathan, Rachel, and Joshua. I do not want Nathan to be kind to Rachel just because he knows the house rules. I want him to help her and encourage her because he loves her. I do not want my home to be a police state where I walk around as the law enforcer.

And I do not want a hierarchy where I am closer to Rachel than I am to Joshua because somehow Rachel might be more intelligent or follows the rules more closely. I do not want a pecking order.

All I want is a family where we do our best to truly love one another and help one another become the best versions of ourselves we can be. I want every one of my children to feel the unshakable, unquestionable security of my love, and in that love to be free.

I also understand the clear boundaries God set up when he said not to eat from the tree of "I will decide for myself what is right and wrong." Nothing can more completely dismantle any hope of having a loving family than everyone deciding for themselves what is right and wrong. If everyone in a family makes themselves the center of the universe and ignores the needs of those around them, chaos ensues.

God's warning to Adam and Eve is completely accurate: if you eat of the Tree of Knowledge of Good and Evil you will surely die. In other words, if I choose self-centered independence, I will unwittingly set in motion my own demise. True relationship requires freedom of choice, definitely. Yet, if I use that freedom for blind self-centeredness, there are real consequences. God's love demanded that he offer the first man and woman freedom and at the same time warn them of the consequences of abusing that freedom.

As a parent, I get this. When I look at God from the perspective of a parent, things start to become a lot clearer. If I were him, I would not want a family obsessed with rules, rituals, or hierarchy either. I would not want religion. All I would want was a place where we could all live together in love, work together in harmony, and grow together in intimacy and in the joy of exploring the world together.

I should not be surprised, then, that all these longings in my heart stem from an innate desire for a perfect world. Death, war, disease, broken relationships, frustration, anger, isolation, and loneliness— everyone, everywhere, in every generation experiences these conditions. But everything in me cries out, "This is all wrong!" My heart longs for that garden experience.

Think about it.

To live in harmony with nature.

To experience heart-to-heart, skin-to-skin intimacy, where I hide nothing, give everything, and experience complete acceptance.

To engage in meaningful and productive work that releases my abilities and creativity as I help to shape a better world.

To share peace with those around me.

To be at one with my Creator and to live as God's friend.

To know the security of a life that never ends.

I hear within me the echo of a perfect world. I have this unshakable desire for divine and human intimacy, for security and meaning, and for a life that never ends. This first act of the story tells me that I carry the imprint of what I was originally created for and that it exists in me for a reason:

It is there like a compass pointing to true north.

It is there to set me on a quest to find my way back home.

Am I in search of the best life possible or am I simply living on autopilot?

3

Broken

Act Two: Genesis 3

ACT TWO OF our story opens with a very persuasive talking serpent on stage. The presence of this odd intruder in our story raises some important questions for us. Where did he come from? How did he find his way into this perfect garden? What role will he play in this unfolding drama?[1] Some of these questions will be answered as the drama unfolds; others will be left for the theologians to debate.

But we do know that the first thing this slippery serpent does upon entering the scene is to slither his way up to Eve and Adam. The serpent wants to plant a simple, insidious thought in Eve's mind: "If you eat from the forbidden tree, you will not die. You will be like God, deciding for yourself what is right and wrong."[2] "Wow!" she must have thought. "Now I can be like God and do anything I want." The lure of independence must have been so appealing. As Eve and Adam listened to the serpent, they must have felt that God was holding something wonderful back from them. Unfortunately, they could not see that they already had all the freedom they needed and could do anything they wanted to do under the care of their loving Father.

But let's be honest with ourselves. All it takes is a series of quick rationalizations and any of us could easily head down a path to a place we do not want to be. Eve quickly comes up with a list of convincing reasons why this particular fruit is exactly what she wants. Like Gollum from *The Lord of the Rings*, she "needs" it. She decides to ignore the warning from her loving Father about the one forbidden tree. She reaches out, picks a luscious piece of fruit, and draws it to her watering mouth. She bites into its sweetness and then turns to Adam, who willingly and without hesitation joins her. He makes his own choice and takes a big bite out of that same piece of destiny-defining fruit.

In an instant their perfect world comes crashing down. Their choice for independence unleashes a completely unexpected consequence: they are now cut off from the one who truly loves them. With one bite, they alienate themselves from the one whose love covered and secured their hearts. Instead of obtaining the freedom and independence they sought, they are now ensnared in a new kind of bondage.

With eyes wide open they now realize how incredibly exposed and vulnerable they are in their nakedness. The nakedness that once represented unashamed intimacy now generates deep fear and embarrassment. They now see they are completely exposed.

Because of their fear and shame, they run for cover. Trembling and shaking, they try to hide in the bushes. Their hearts, now permanently gripped by fear, are bent inward. No longer are they selfless. Instead of looking for ways to love God and each other, all they can think of now are their own needs.

As Act Two continues, we see their pathetic attempt to rescue themselves from their plight and protect their hearts from this new sense of exposure. They string together some leaves as a pitiful covering for their nakedness. Then they crouch behind some bushes and tremble at the thought of being found out.

> When the cool evening breezes were blowing, the man and his wife heard the LORD God walking about in the garden. So they hid from the LORD God among the trees. Then the LORD God called to the man, "Where are you?"

He replied, "I heard you walking in the garden, so I hid. I was afraid because I was naked."

"Who told you that you were naked?" the LORD God asked. "Have you eaten from the tree whose fruit I commanded you not to eat?"

The man replied, "It was the woman you gave me who gave me the fruit, and I ate it."

Then the LORD God asked the woman, "What have you done?"

"The serpent deceived me," she replied. "That's why I ate it."

GENESIS 3:8-13, NLT

Soon, it is the cool of the day — the best time to relax with friends — and God comes looking for his companions. "Where are you?" he calls out. This is not some aloof God of ancient myth waiting on his distant throne in heaven to judge and condemn. Rather, this scene reveals a caring Father who relentlessly seeks his lost and lonely children in the woods.

As the Creator's shadow passes by where they are crouching, Adam, overcome with a sense of failure and shame, meekly cries out, "I was afraid because I was naked; so I hid." He knows it is time to come clean and make his confession.

In Adam's confession, "I was afraid because I was naked; so I hid," we get an important window into the broken human condition. In this simple statement, we hear the crippling fear that also consumes many of us when we become aware that we have missed the mark, failed, or outright rebelled. We also get a sense of the complete vulnerability, exposure, embarrassment, and shame that comes when we know we are not the person we should be, or can be.

The fear that gripped the first man and woman drove them to try to desperately save themselves. The first thing they do is to try and hide their true selves. Instead of going directly to God, toward the light, toward the one who could help them, they stop trusting in God's character and rely on their own remedies. They cover up and look inward for a solution—one that ends up distancing them from God and from each other.

Are we any different from Adam and Eve? In our failure and fear of exposure, do not we too sometimes run, hide, and try to cover up? I know I do. Many of us distance ourselves from God and others when we fail because we are afraid of being exposed. Yet we need to do just the opposite. We need to run toward those who love us with open hearts so we can find help and healing.

Are there places in my life where I am hiding my true self from God or others?

As we get back to the scene unfolding on stage, we notice that God gets right to the point and asks the hard and honest question. "Did you eat from the forbidden tree?" In their answers, we see another terrible consequence of self-centeredness: blame. Adam's answer to God's question is accusatory: "The woman *you* put here with me—*she* gave me some fruit from the tree, and I ate it" (emphasis added). Notice that he not only blames his wife, but insinuates that God is ultimately to blame for the whole mess.

Eve's response is not much better: "The serpent deceived me." Now, apparently, the serpent is entirely to blame. Neither Adam nor Eve takes responsibility for what happens. They attempt to deflect, redirect, and avoid the issue. Blame and anger now replace mutual trust, love, and submission. In addition to the leaves covering their bodies, Adam and Eve try and cover up what they did by pointing fingers at each other, each trying to deflect attention away from what they have done.

How much are we like that? How do we hide ourselves, deflect blame, and rationalize our bad choices? Do we fight for our own safety even if it means attacking someone else or shifting blame? I am pretty sure you know what the answer is.

Fear and shame lead to anger and blame, and we will discover in this story that hiding and accusing eventually lead to stealing and killing. The choice of "I will decide for myself what is right and wrong" unleashes a monster that will haunt humanity for ages to come.

As the second act comes to a close, the first man and woman come face-to-face with the consequences of their rejection of God. Due to their lack of trust in his goodness, the garden is now closed to them. They are forced to step into a world marred and broken, and face the many choices that come with it.

God now explains the curses that will fall on Adam and Eve and their descendants as a result of what they have done. Their labour will be forever filled with pain and toil. Relationships will be filled with struggle. These curses are not about some cruel and unusual punishment that God will actively inflict on them. Rather, they represent an accurate description of what Adam and Eve must now face, given the unwise choice they made in the garden. The natural order of life and creation will be bound by suffering and pain. Relationships will be forever marked by competition and conflict. Eventually, life will come to an end. Both man and woman, in their frailty, will return to dust. These are the inevitable consequences of going your own way.

Yet the first man and woman are not left without hope. God gives them something beautiful to hold on to. He promises that one day a descendant of the woman will come to humanity as a rescuer and deliverer. This rescuer, at the cost of intense suffering, will deal a final, deadly blow to evil once and for all.[3]

So the Lord God said to the serpent, "Because you have done this,

> "Cursed are you above all livestock
>   and all wild animals!
> You will crawl on your belly
>   and you will eat dust
>   all the days of your life.
> And I will put enmity
>   between you and the woman,

and between your offspring and hers;
he will crush your head,
    and you will strike his heel."

To the woman he said,

"I will make your pains in childbearing very severe;
    with painful labor you will give birth to children.
Your desire will be for your husband,
    and he will rule over you. "

To Adam he said, "Because you listened to your wife and ate fruit from the tree about which I commanded you, 'You must not eat from it,'

Cursed is the ground because of you;
    through painful toil you will eat food from it
    all the days of your life.
It will produce thorns and thistles for you,
    and you will eat the plants of the field.
By the sweat of your brow
    you will eat your food
until you return to the ground,
    since from it you were taken;
for dust you are
    and to dust you will return."

GENESIS 3:14-19

As an act of both grace and judgment, God does one last thing at the end of Act Two that speaks volumes. He kills two animals and makes garments of skin from them, which Adam and Eve are to wear in place of the leaves that they had stitched together to cover themselves. This act of extreme grace symbolizes his commitment to cover their shame. God himself provides a covering for their exposure that is better than anything they can make for themselves. But the price is high — the price of blood. In this vivid picture, human failure claims its first death, a death that would foreshadow an even greater sacrifice to come.

At the end of this act, the woman and man step out of the garden, newly clothed, into a fallen world, to await this Promised One who would undo the mess they had created. Could the lost dream be restored?

Do I think this world is working the way I think it should?

Are there parts of me that are not working right?

Do I feel connected to God or disconnected from God (if I believe God exists)?

Reflection on Broken

I sometimes think that the latest news headlines would make great taglines for horror movies:

"Rebel forces execute helpless hostages."

"Gunman kills ten children in shooting spree."

"Oil spill destroys habitat."

"HIV/AIDS responsible for millions of impoverished orphans."

"Destruction of the rainforest continues unabated."

Agent Smith, in the movie *The Matrix*, has a great monologue about humanity that seems fitting when we think about all the evil things that humans do in the world. As part of a computer-controlled virtual universe, Smith saw a free humanity as an impediment to the goal of maintaining a perfect world. In his pressed suit and dark sunglasses, he states to Morpheus, a leader of the human resistance, that he has had a revelation. Smith, with carefully measured words, states that he has come to realize that humans are not mammals. He explains his rationale. All mammals instinctively and naturally find a balance and equilibrium with their environment whereas humans continue to multiply, spread, and consume the resources around them until they have depleted everything in their environment. He then pauses and asks the obvious. What other organism on earth follows this pattern? He answers his own question and in doing so, provides the rationale for his mission to exterminate humans: "A virus. Human beings are a disease, a cancer of this planet. You're a plague and we are the cure.[4]"

I do not think Agent Smith has the cure for what is wrong with humanity. And I do not think that we need to share his ultimate view of humanity. Yet, from one perspective, there is truth in what he says. It is easy to feel grief, anger, and disgust when we look at what is happening in our world. Even though we have caused most of it, we mourn the suffering and pain of our planet.

I clearly remember the funeral of a six-year-old boy who had died of cancer. My oldest son was six at the time. I just did not get it. As I looked at my own son's health and vitality, I could see how amazing life was meant to be. As I stood with the devastated mom and dad beside their son's casket, my heart ached with the thought, "This is wrong."

Disease and natural disasters are hardwired into this planet, and yet we sense that this was not how it was meant to be. Even though we constantly face examples of human imperfection and a broken natural order, most of us see the imprint of perfection behind it all. We sense that something has been corrupted, that something has gone terribly wrong. Just as the story of the garden helps us to make sense of our longing for a perfect world, the failure of Adam and Eve helps us to make sense of why the world is so screwed up. The curses God speaks out to Adam and Eve make it clear that the natural order is broken; a spiritual disease has spread throughout all creation, infecting everything, and I mean everything.

But there is more. The story of Adam and Eve also explains why I am so screwed up.

You see, this is not ultimately just our first parents' story. This is my story. This is our story. It is the one story every single descendant of our first parents repeats as they live out their own stories.

Here I discover that the human heart so easily chooses selfish independence over humble and loving submission. Pride sneaks into our hearts and convinces us to judge for ourselves what will be good and evil.

What did the serpent say to deceive Eve? He said, "You will be like God, knowing good and evil" (Genesis 3:5).

There it is. If I am honest with myself, there is a part of me that wants to be the god of my own little world. Like Eve and Adam gazing at the forbidden fruit, I want what I want when I want it. We all want to judge for ourselves what is good and evil; we all want to decide for ourselves what is right and wrong.

But this selfish independence comes with inescapable consequences. Adam confessed, "I was afraid because I was naked; so I hid." Here we see that the first and most immediate consequence is fear.

We inherently feel the vulnerability of our independence. When we are cut off from God, we cannot help but realize we are nothing but tiny little creatures trying to stand up against forces in this world that are much more powerful than anything we possess. Our hearts know this.

As we isolate ourselves from God and other people, we become afraid. And we should be. We are left with only our own strength and ingenuity to save us. Like Adam and Eve hiding in the bushes, we have discovered a million ways to medicate our fears and hide our true selves. Just check out any magazine rack at a local convenience store. Complete makeovers, the latest fashions, tips for securing that promotion at work, the car of your dreams, the perfect house—an endless list of ways to improve how we present ourselves and make our world appear more secure.

Yet, why do so many who seem to have it all—beautiful models, powerful business leaders, successful athletes—fall prey to depression, drugs, and even suicide? It does not take a rocket scientist to figure this out. The perfect body, the most prestigious position, the greatest wealth, the most valued possessions—none of these can ultimately satisfy or secure our hearts. Possessions may quiet our fears for a time, but before long the insecurity returns. We need to stop and ask ourselves, "What happens if I lose what I have? Can any of this keep me from dying one day?"

Having come from the dust of the earth, our "dustness" seems inescapable. Maybe when we are younger we can live in denial about death. However, the older we get, the more it creeps up on us. It does not matter how much we run on the treadmill or cake on the anti-wrinkle cream, whether it is today or in the future, our tombstones cast giant shadows over our lives. Whether it is the sight of grey hairs on our heads, being diagnosed with a terminal disease, or hearing news that a friend has died, deep down we all know that the clock is ticking on our mortality and there is nothing we can do about it.

Inescapable fear is not the only emotional consequence of our independence and isolation. Fear almost always leads us to anger.

Adam and Eve first tasted isolation as they hid in their fear. But right away, their fear and shame ignited into anger and blame. When we do not get what we want, our self-centered nature immediately looks for someone to be the scapegoat for our unhappiness. Whether it is a school-yard scrap, a painful divorce, or a bloody war between nations, our fear of getting hurt fuels our anger toward any who might threaten us. Whether we hurl cutting words, throw bloody fists, or launch deadly missiles, the cause is the same. My drive to secure myself means I am tempted to do whatever is necessary to make sure that I am okay and get what I want, even if it means some-one else suffers.

This comes out in family settings most clearly. Grab what you want as soon as you can. Point the finger when something goes wrong. If someone protests, shout as loud as you can. If someone gets in your face, push them out of the way (and if you think that is bad, you should see how the kids act).

Seriously, though, adults are just like kids when it comes to anger and blame; we are just better at dressing it up with sophistication and wit. We have our tactics: the carefully crafted barbs laced into our con-versations, the quiet sabotage to ensure our perceived competitor fails, the criticisms carefully calculated to place those we do not like in the worst possible light. We skillfully use blame games and power plays to vent our anger and defend our interests. This is what self-centeredness does to the human heart. This is what it does to me.

As dark as this all seems, the second act of this grand story reveals that unfortunately the negative consequences of our selfish choices do not stop here. Our self-centeredness has become the most destructive force on the planet. Put aside the natural disasters and diseases for a moment. Stop and consider what human self-interest has done to this world: systematic oppression of the weak, slavery, endless war, genocide, widespread pollution, unbridled destruction of our natural resources. The worst stuff that happens on the planet cannot be blamed on nature or God. It rests at the feet of the human race.

Furthermore, our rebellious self-centeredness has damaged our relationship with God. This should come as no big surprise. Although God desires true friendship, he is completely perfect. In keeping with his perfect nature he must bring all evil to judgment. The trajectory our first parents set by their rebellion has now positioned us as God's enemies, and so we, like Adam and Eve, are now under the divine judgment called death. This should not surprise us, because he told us from the beginning that this path would lead only to death. So now we see death everywhere. You cannot escape it. I cannot escape it.

However, as the curtain falls on the end of the second act, we are not left without hope. The God of perfection is also a God of incredible mercy and grace. God gives humanity something that we can hold on to, something that can give us hope in the midst of our brokenness. He has given us a promise. He said that someone would eventually come and deliver a final, deadly blow to evil and to the mysterious serpent who initiated it all back in the garden. Somehow, in some way, he will rescue us from the deadly choices we have made.

Surprisingly, there is no "if . . . then" statement attached to this promise. God did not say, "*If* you go through such-and-such religious ritual or process of purification or enlightenment, *then* I will send a rescuer to save you." No. God committed himself to rescue humanity on his own, without qualifications. Adam and Eve did not even ask him to do this. Although God's nature of perfect goodness demands that he judge the evil we have created, God's nature of rich grace means that he will also be the one who will rescue us.

As Act Two of our story draws to a close, we are left to wonder:

Who is this rescuer?

Who will rescue us from ourselves and our self-centeredness?

Who will save us from trying to save ourselves?

And, after we have ruined his perfect world and rejected him outright, could God still love us? Even if I have messed up in a huge way, could he love me that much?

4

Struggle

Act Three: Genesis 4 to Malachi

Scene One

AS WE HAVE seen previously, one characteristic of self-centeredness is that we tend to think we know what is best. We start to believe that if we can find the right environment, situation, or circumstance, then we will become the good people we long to be and start to live the good life we want. But is this really true?

Act Three tells the story of the small, nomadic group of people called Israel. Their story is essentially the story of "what does not work" to change the human heart and restore intimacy with God. Act Three moves through four major scenes. Each comes with a powerful lesson, and all of them are pretty much the opposite of what we expect God would want to show humanity. We discover, through this ancient case study, that we humans need something much more than a good environment in order to be good people and live a good life. We need our hearts changed from the inside out.

The first scene of the third act picks up where Act Two left off. In the garden were two trees that offered Adam and Eve two choices, two ways to live. They chose the wrong one. However, as we move forward in the story, we realize that these same two choices remain for humanity. First, there is the self-determined way: the "I'll decide for myself" way. This way may look good in the beginning, but, as we will see, eventually goes disastrously wrong. Then there is God's way, which may look ridiculous from a human point of view, but ultimately ends up being the very best way.

As we move through Act Three, we encounter character after character that reinforces the basic truth that you cannot judge by appearances. Only God knows what is in the human heart, and only God knows what is ultimately best.

Consider Adam and Eve's sons, Cain and Abel.[1] Abel trusts God so much that he gives God the best of what he has. What fool gives away his very best? Cain, on the other hand, gives God what he can afford. Guess which one is blessed? From a human point of view, Cain looks like the wiser of the two brothers, giving to God out of the extra he can afford. But God was more interested in their hearts than their offerings.

Abel trusted and loved God so much that he wanted to give the very best he had. Cain was subtly looking out for number one. Guess which one goes murderously crazy with envy when he sees he is not blessed by God? Cain's murder of Abel gives us a vivid picture of how deadly a selfish heart can be. A simple bite of forbidden fruit escalates to murder in the space of one generation. Yikes!

Two other stories, one about Noah and the other about the people of Babel, also exemplify how God does not care about appearances but looks at our hearts.[2] Both are about building projects, but with opposite outcomes.

To the people of his time, Noah seemed like someone who was off his rocker. He spends a lot of time building a massive boat in a place where there is virtually no water and very little rain because he believes a catastrophic flood is coming. He trusts God in a radical way. He is willing to do what God asks him to do and ends up looking like a fool because he believes what God has told him. In response, God uses him to save the known world.[3]

The story of Babel has a much different outcome. Here we find a large group of people attempting to construct the world's biggest tower. However, they are doing it to put their pride and wisdom on display. They think they can climb all the way up to God. Talk about arrogance. But their pride brings judgment from God. He shuts down the building project by making them speak different languages. Suddenly, no one can understand his neighbor. And where there is no communication, there can be no real relationship or partnership. The people of Babel look so wise in their ability to build a magnificent tower, but in the end, the pride in their hearts leads to a disunity, division, and dispersion that still plagues the human race.

With each unfolding story[4] of Act Three we see a pattern. Those who do things God's way appear totally crazy, yet things work out in unexpected and good ways for them. Those who do things their own way, however, as wise as it may seem at first, end up in a complete mess.

Do I think that my own approach to life is truly the best way to live?

Or could there be another way, one that may look foolish to me now but in the end would be better?

The key figure in this first scene of the third act is a guy named Abram, also called Abraham, who lives in the land of Canaan. God has a promise to keep and so he needs to start somewhere. He begins with a vision to create a new community that will be known as the people of God. When God looks for someone from whom to build a whole new community, does he choose a person from one of the ancient palaces? Nope. He picks a guy out in the middle of nowhere, a guy with no permanent address.

At first, Abram is an absolute nobody, but he ends up becoming a best friend of God. What qualifies him for this privileged status? His elevated status does not flow from strict observance of religious rituals or regulations. He simply trusts God as a committed friend.

Some time later, the LORD spoke to Abram in a vision and said to him, "Do not be afraid, Abram, for I will protect you, and your reward will be great."

But Abram replied, "O Sovereign LORD, what good are all your blessings when I don't even have a son? Since you've given me no children, Eliezer of Damascus, a servant in my household, will inherit all my wealth. You have given me no descendants of my own, so one of my servants will be my heir."

Then the LORD said to him, "No, your servant will not be your heir, for you will have a son of your own who will be your heir." Then the LORD took Abram outside and said to him, "Look up into the sky and count the stars if you can. That's how many descendants you will have!"

And Abram believed the LORD, and the LORD counted him as righteous because of his faith.

GENESIS 15:1-6, NLT

Here is the story in brief. Abram, now in his old age and with no children, enters into a trust-based covenant relationship[5] with God. It is not a contract. It is not a bargain. It is a life-and-death commitment from God to fulfill a promise. It is love formalized.

God knows that a lifelong covenant is the only way to sustain and nurture a close, loving relationship. Individuals, families, or communities who would experience and share God's true love must be rooted in the security of a covenant.

As part of his covenant with Abram, God makes an incredible promise. He tells Abram that he and his aged wife Sarai will have a son whose descendants will one day grow into a great nation with their own land. To drive the point home, God even changes their names to Abraham, meaning "Father of many," and Sarah, meaning "mother of nations." What unfolds after Abraham receives this promise is a story[6] that takes the concept of trust to a whole new level.

At an extreme old age, Abraham and Sarah miraculously have a son. They name him Isaac. God then does the unthinkable. He asks Abraham to sacrifice his son back to God. That's right. God asks Abram to kill his only son on an altar as an act of worship. This request goes against everything we know or will come to know about God. It appears to completely contradict the promise God gave to Abram about having descendants who would become a great nation.

It is wrong in every conceivable way.

Abraham obviously does not understand why God would ask something so horrifying, but he knows he can trust God. He goes all the way to the point of building an altar and raising a knife to the throat of his son before God stops the test. In this, Abram demonstrates, beyond any shadow of a doubt, that he trusts God, even when it looks completely insane.

This is an appalling and disturbing story for most of us. But it makes a point we should not forget: to trust God means that we trust him in everything—absolutely everything.

God now declares that Abraham is righteous. In other words, Abraham has a right standing before God or is in a right relationship with him. Why? God says this about Abraham because of one thing: he trusts God. Abraham was not declared righteous by God because he was legalistically religious or profoundly enlightened. Quite the contrary, you probably would not have found a more average guy in the whole Middle East. Abraham simply trusts God, and this trust qualifies him to become the father of a family, a community that would be called to live by that one key idea: trust. To be a friend of God you must trust God more than anything or anyone, even more than you trust yourself—even when it looks completely crazy.

At this point in my life, who do I trust more, me or God (if you believe God exists)?

Abram's story teaches us a lot about trust. But as we move on, we also learn that this idea of trusting God is a struggle for everyone. Isaac, Abraham's promised son, grows up and himself has two sons, Esau and

Jacob.[7] Now Jacob, the youngest, is a real character. He is the kind of guy you just love to hate. He is manipulative and deceptive and, quite honestly, a jerk. But here comes God again with the unexpected. God has good plans for Jacob.

Jacob spends much of his life grasping and clutching for everything he wants. Does he trust God? Definitely not like his grandpa Abraham. In time, all of Jacob's grabby greed catches up to him. He has deceived his brother one too many times. He is alone in the middle of nowhere, and his brother Esau, with all of his men, is descending on him. It is the middle of the night, and Jacob fearfully awaits his impending confrontation with Esau. Suddenly, in the black of the night, a mysterious figure sneaks up on Jacob and jumps him. Who could this be? Jacob wrestles with this guy all night long, struggling for his life.

When this mysterious figure realizes that Jacob will not submit, he demonstrates his incredible power by a simple touch that miraculously throws Jacob's hip bone out of joint. Searing pain rips through Jacob's body. Now Jacob can no longer clutch and grab out of greed and control. All he can do now is cling for dear life. In his agonizing brokenness, he realizes he is wrestling with the Divine. Completely desperate, he hangs on and begs God to bless him. However, God is not overcome by Jacob's pathetic attempt to control him. God's power is too great for that. Rather, God's heart is overcome by Jacob's humble brokenness and desperation.

In this wrestling match with God we find a profound truth. In our pride, we often try to control our own lives and get what we want by grabbing what we can. Like Jacob, if we stick with this approach, we are in danger of losing everything. Yet, if we hang on to God and allow him to break our stubborn hearts, that breaking will be our healing. Like Jacob, once we are broken we will discover God's true blessing and calling on our lives.

That night, God changes his name from Jacob, which means "deceiver," to "Israel," which means one who "struggles with God." The next morning Jacob is walking with a limp, a permanent reminder that he wrestled with God and was both broken and healed in the process.

Israel, the one who struggles with God, becomes the father of a family that, in time, will bring fulfillment of the promise made to Abraham. Eventually, he will have twelve sons and, in the most tangible way, the promise of a nation will begin.

These twelve sons will be the founding fathers of the twelve tribes of Israel, a nation-sized family. As we will soon see, God wisely names this nation "Israel," or "one who struggles with God." Forget the glowing success stories. Nothing will come easily to these people. Every step of the journey will be a battle. Yet in all of this, we will see God revealing the truth we all need to see.

Where am I wrestling with life right now?

What is driving me in this struggle?

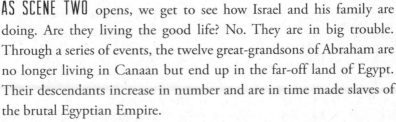

5

Religion

Act Three: Scene Two

AS SCENE TWO opens, we get to see how Israel and his family are doing. Are they living the good life? No. They are in big trouble. Through a series of events, the twelve great-grandsons of Abraham are no longer living in Canaan but end up in the far-off land of Egypt. Their descendants increase in number and are in time made slaves of the brutal Egyptian Empire.

During this time, starting with the birth of their leader Moses to the end of a period called "Judges," God rescues the descendants of Israel from slavery and leads them all to a land they can call their own. This is the land promised to their ancestor Abraham and so is rightly called the Promised Land.

Now, during this journey from Egypt to their Promised Land, there is a plot twist. The God of friendship and simple trust gives the people of Israel a complex religion. Why would God do this? This religion (or system of salvation) is unlike any religion known to humanity. Is it possible that it has the power to change the human heart and enable these former slaves to live in a right relationship with God?[1] Good question. We will see.

Now, back to the story.[2] The people of Israel are enslaved in Egypt, and God needs to send them a rescuer. So where does God go looking for one? You guessed it. He goes out to the middle of nowhere and finds a simple man who looks after sheep. A man named Moses.

So who is this guy Moses? Moses did not start his life as a humble shepherd. His life begins with a lot of promise. Although originally born in Egypt to an Israelite slave, Moses is adopted by one of Pharaoh's daughters when he is a tiny baby. Raised in a life of privilege and success, his life takes a serious turn for the worse when, as a young man, he kills an Egyptian in a foolish attempt to defend his own enslaved and suffering people. He then runs for his life.

Yet, even in the midst of this great failure, God has big plans for Moses. Many years later, he finds Moses in the desert, watching sheep for his father-in-law Jethro. God meets with Moses on a mountain[3] and uses a burning bush to get his attention. He then tells him that he has a mission for him. God wants to use Moses to rescue the Israelites from Egypt. He wants to start a committed relationship with the Israelites and lead them to the land promised to their ancestors Abraham, Isaac, and Jacob.

Of course Moses comes up with a lot of questions and reasons why this is not a good idea. One of his biggest objections is that he is a lousy public speaker. But God's assurances help him overcome his doubts and insecurities, and so he decides to trust God and accept this mission. Armed with just a stick in hand and God as his friend, Moses marches into Egypt to take on the most powerful nation on the planet at the time. Remember, trusting God will sometimes make you look crazy.

This leads to an Old-West style showdown between Moses and Pharaoh. With Moses and his stick, now called "the staff of God," God decisively demonstrates the magnitude of his divine power. Again and again, Moses raises the "staff of God" and in response, God unleashes a series of gross and deadly plagues to show, without a doubt, that he is more powerful than all the gods of Egypt's religion put together.

On the night of the final and most deadly plague, God tells Moses to have all the Israelites gather as families and share a special last meal in Egypt. Each element of the meal symbolizes their story as a people. They are instructed to take some blood from the lamb they would eat and paint it on their door frames so that they would be passed over by the angel of God's judgment. Blood would be an enduring symbol of God's provision of salvation. As with Adam and Eve and the sacrifice made for their clothing, innocent blood was shed again so that Israel could be covered, protected, and saved.

The meal they ate that fateful night, the night God's judgment passed over them and they were delivered, is called the Passover. From then on, the Israelites would share this meal once a year to remember what God had done in rescuing them. God wants his people to remember their shared story, and so he seals this important event with a meaningful way for the story to be remembered and retold to future generations.

This final plague is more than Pharaoh can handle and so he lets the Israelites go. With victory now in hand and God's people released from pharaoh's grip, Moses leads the people miraculously through the Red Sea into the desert. They leave Pharaoh and the Egyptians mourning their disastrous attempt to oppose God.

However, before these newly-freed Israelites are allowed to meet with God to sort out what it means to be his people, they must march through a dry and difficult wilderness for a few months. This is a kind of boot camp that tests the people to see what is really in their hearts. Do they trust God even when things are tough? Or will they quickly resort to doing things their own way? It becomes clear that even after God has miraculously rescued them, they still refuse to trust him.[4] Just like their first parents, Adam and Eve, they want to decide for themselves what is right and wrong rather than simply trust God.

Eventually, Moses leads the people to a mountain called Sinai to set up a nationwide covenant[5] with God, similar to the one established with their ancestor Abraham. But because the people do not trust God fully, this covenant is different. It is not an unconditional covenant flowing from a tested and proven trust-based relationship like the one established with Abraham.[6] In this conditional covenant God basically says, "*If* you obey my commands, *then* you will be my people."

God lays down the Law and clearly defines how the nation should live. Like a parent putting a defiant toddler in a playpen, God puts up clear boundaries and expectations around Israel to keep them on track. God has a plan he intends to complete, even if the descendants of Abraham do not get it. He has a promise to keep to an old friend.

So here in the wilderness Israel gets religion. God gives them rules for what they should and should not do if they are going to be his people. Now before we unpack what God put into this religion, we have to zero in on ten rules in particular, which are the centerpiece of the religion. These are the Ten Commandments[7] that were carved by God on two stone tablets.

The first five commands deal with their relationship with God:
No other gods.
No idols of other gods.
Do not misuse God's name.
Keep the Sabbath, God's day to rest.
Honor your mother and father, God's authorities in your life.
The second five deal with their relationship with their neighbors:
Do not murder your neighbor.
Do not commit adultery with your neighbor's spouse.
Do not steal from your neighbor.
Do not give false testimony against your neighbor.
Do not even covet your neighbor's stuff.

Each list of five begins with the most severe and obvious offenses and then progresses to the least obvious offense. In a sense, each list of five goes, if we are thinking in colors, from black to light grey, from external to internal, from "what I do in my actions" to "the thoughts and intents of my heart."

The Ten Commandments are not an arbitrary collection of rules, but rather a way to examine our relationships. They are a gauge that measures our destructive self-centeredness. They are not a cure but a diagnostic tool.

God calls his people to reflect on the Ten Commandments day and night so that they can live other-centered lives. If we want to understand why God gave them religion, we must grasp the significance of this diagnostic tool. God knew he needed to drive home a single point, both for the Israelites and for all the rest of us. Here it is: we all have heart issues. The many things we do against God and each other all come from one source: our hearts.

What are the motivations of my heart?

Now beyond these Ten Commandments, what else did God include in the package? This religion has five basic elements.

First, he gives his people a long list of additional rules that would govern virtually every detail of their daily lives. Externally, these rules remind the Israelites over and over again that they are to live lives set apart to God. These rules describe, in exacting detail, a form of justice, compassion, and righteousness that was radical compared to their cultural context.

Second, God delineates a clear process for offering sacrifices when his people mess up, so that they can be forgiven. These sacrifices regularly remind the Israelites that sin breaks covenant relationships and ultimately brings death. Yet they also remind them that God is a gracious and forgiving God who wants to provide a way to restore people who have broken relationship and fallen short.

Third, God initiates nationwide festivals and traditions to remind the people of their rich story and epic journey with God. They are never to forget that they were once slaves who were miraculously saved by God. These festivals are reminders of how grateful they should be that God has chosen, loved, and rescued them despite their weakness and humble beginnings.

Fourth, God installs a group of spiritual leaders called priests, who would serve as mediators between God and this family. It was the priests' role to keep everyone on track within this religion.

Finally, God directs the people to make a special tent for him called the tabernacle. God's plan was to go camping with them wherever they went, showing them just how important having a relationship with them was to him. God wants to be with us just like he walked in the garden with our first parents, Adam and Eve.

This all sounds pretty good, yes?

Within this religion we see many important values. God wants to be close to his people. He wants to forgive their failures and sins. He wants the poor and vulnerable protected. He wants to help people maintain healthy relationships in their homes and communities. He wants people to work together to help each other.

Compared to the practices and religions of other major ancient civilizations, this code of conduct and the value it places on human life is remarkable. Laws are put in place to protect the most vulnerable members of society—among them, women, servants, and the poor. Ritual prostitution and human sacrifice, widely practiced at this time, are strictly forbidden. Limitations are placed on how long a property can be rented to another person. This way, every family is guaranteed the security of land and the ability to provide for itself. Within its own time and culture, this Law promoted a new and higher level of mercy and justice.[8]

In a very real way, the Israelites, as a family, had the potential to be a bright light to those around them. This new religious system provided them with a thousand and one daily, weekly, and yearly reminders of their high calling as God's people. With all these reminders, how could they ever forget to do the right thing? One would think that with an entire nation rallying together, they would be set for life. Yet, in time, we see this is far from the case.

Now, there are two more surprises to the whole religious deal God sets up.

First, when he finishes giving the Law to the Israelites God tells Moses that keeping the Law will not work to change their hearts.[9] In fact, God tells Moses to write down a song for the people to sing as a reminder that the Law ultimately will not work and, further, that they will break this covenant with God. God knows what is in the human heart and what it is disposed to do. God knows that this Law is bound to fail from the start. Why, then, would God give the Law if he knows it will fail? As we will see, God has a plan. There is an ultimate solution coming, but the Law, although it is a part of the plan, is not the solution.

> Now write down this song and teach it to the Israelites and have them sing it, so that it may be a witness for me against them. When I have brought them into the land flowing with milk and honey, the land I promised on oath to their ancestors, and when they eat their fill and thrive, they will turn to other gods and worship them, rejecting me and breaking my covenant. And when many disasters and calamities come on them, this song will testify against them, because it will not be forgotten by their descendants. I know what they are disposed to do, even before I bring them into the land I promised them on oath.
>
> DEUTERONOMY 31:19-21

There is a second surprise. Moses, who gives the people of Israel all these rules (called the Torah or the Law), actually has a much more intimate and personal relationship with God than any of the rituals and rules suggest.[10] He lives like a friend of God, talking to him whenever he wants. He is more like Abraham, just hanging out with God, and less like some religious legalist thumping a big rule book. Strange, isn't it? The guy God uses to give all the rules to the people should have to follow all of the rules, yes? In fact, he should be the best at keeping the rules, right? No, Moses does not have to follow all of the rules. He is simply a friend. This suggests that there is a better way to live with God than being addicted to rules.

These two surprises are clues that God is setting up something special. He has a higher plan.

> Whenever Moses went out to the Tent of Meeting, all the people would get up and stand in the entrances of their own tents. They would all watch Moses until he disappeared inside. As he went into the tent, the pillar of cloud would come down and hover at its entrance while the Lord spoke with Moses. When the people saw the cloud standing at the entrance of the tent, they would stand and bow down in front of their own tents. Inside the Tent of Meeting, the Lord would speak to Moses face to face, as one speaks to a friend.
>
> Exodus 33:8-11, NLT

After God gives the people of Israel the laws and the basis of their new "religion," he leads them on to a beautiful place where they can have their own space and no one can bother or tempt them. It is the Promised Land. A military leader named Joshua, the successor of Moses, leads them in conquest to claim this land as their own.

By the end of this second scene, the people are secure in the land. They know exactly what the good life looks like. They have all the rules. They even have a way to be forgiven if they mess up. And, if in doubt, they have a whole group of religiously smart guys called priests to ask questions of.

So, are they living the dream? Far from it.

The concluding statement of this scene is telling: "All the people did whatever seemed right in their own eyes" (Judges 17:6; 21:25, NLT).[11] Sound familiar? They are right back to deciding for themselves what is right and wrong. With all this, they are still completely absorbed in their own self-centered, self-destructive ways. They have all the rules and all the space they need, but they still have an inescapable problem. Their hearts are bent and broken. That is something they cannot escape from.

Aside from any rules God may give, do I even follow my own rules? If not, why do I not live up to the rules I make for myself?

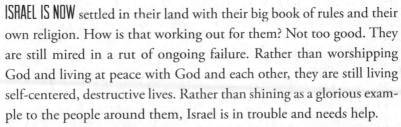

6

Kingdom

Act Three: Scene Three

ISRAEL IS NOW settled in their land with their big book of rules and their own religion. How is that working out for them? Not too good. They are still mired in a rut of ongoing failure. Rather than worshipping God and living at peace with God and each other, they are still living self-centered, destructive lives. Rather than shining as a glorious example to the people around them, Israel is in trouble and needs help.

The people of Israel now decide to look to the surrounding nations for some inspiration and self-improvement tips. They start to say stuff like: "Hey! These other nations have kings to keep them in line. We also need a king to keep us in line." But God has already made it crystal clear that he does not want them to have a king. He wants to be their one true King. But do they listen? By now you can guess the answer. Nope. They insist on having a king.

Apparently, they do not want God's rule anymore. They want to take care of themselves. From their perspective, a strong, top-down leader looks like the best way to go. It is human nature, isn't it? We want a strong, powerful hero to save us from our problems.

This third scene opens with Israel getting their first king, a man named Saul. This scene teaches us what happens when Israel rejects God as their leader and looks for a mere human to lead them. This part of our larger story is essentially a case study of four different kinds of leaders. It helps us see the dark side of each leadership style and illustrates why it is only God whom we can truly trust to lead us into a new life.

Case Study One: Saul, Israel's first king, is a typical Type A leader who stands head-and-shoulders above his peers. He mobilizes the military and quickly makes the nation's borders secure. But does this powerhouse of a leader keep Israel in line with God's purposes? No. Saul fails. He ends up a paranoid, demonized maniac whom God ultimately rejects in favor of a shepherd boy who plays the harp. So much for putting a tough guy in charge.

Case Study Two: the pendulum now swings to the other side. David is a soft-hearted, humble king. He trusts God deeply, in a way that puts him in league with other great friends of God, like Moses and Abraham. He has the incredible faith to take on a giant, Goliath, whom he defeats with a stone and sling instead of a shield and sword. He has incredible respect for those in leadership (even when they are trying to kill him). He is even artsy. In his spare time he plays the harp and writes songs that express his sensitive side to God.

As king, David's heart for God shines. He is inspired to transform Israel's place of worship, from the humble tent of meeting called the tabernacle to a large, beautiful temple. God responds to David's heart and vision for the temple by offering David a trust-based covenant relationship like God had with Abraham and Moses. In this covenant, God promises David that his son will build the temple. More importantly, God promises David that he will have a descendant who will establish an everlasting kingdom.

Could this future king be the coming rescuer? What an amazing promise of hope for this soft-hearted, humble king.

But before you know it, the humble king goes too far. Rather than grabbing on to God's promise and setting a stellar example of obedience to God, David starts to relax in his kingly comfort. At one point, he decides not to join the troops in battle as their leader and instead stays back in the safety and luxury of his palace. He then commits adultery with a beautiful woman named Bathsheba, who, in turn, becomes pregnant.

The beautiful Bathsheba is married to one of David's decorated military officers. To make matters worse, David orders one of his commanders to send this officer into a battle that will virtually ensure he gets killed. The now-powerful king thinks he can cover up his wrongdoing with Bathsheba. He does not get away with it though. God sends the prophet Nathan to confront David, who then comes clean. Brokenhearted, David seeks God's forgiveness.

His tragic lack of judgment, along with other examples of abdication and indecision, leaves David's legacy marred by failure. Despite all this, God continues to have a close relationship with David, and from his family line will come God's promised rescuer.

Let's now consider one of David's great insights about God, captured in one of the songs he wrote, Psalm 51.

> Have mercy on me, O God,
>   because of your unfailing love.
> Because of your great compassion,
>   blot out the stain of my sins.
> Wash me clean from my guilt.
>   Purify me from my sin . . .
> Create in me a clean heart, O God.
>   Renew a loyal spirit within me . . .
> You do not desire a sacrifice, or I would offer one.
>   You do not want a burnt offering.
> The sacrifice you desire is a broken spirit.
>   You will not reject a broken and repentant heart, O God.
>
> PSALM 51:1-2,10,16-17, NLT

What do we learn from this song by David, the king God describes as "a man after his own heart" (1 Samuel 13:14). Although it was written after he had committed adultery and murder, David declares that

God does not care about the religious system at all. What God cares about is a humble heart. Only when people have humble hearts will the outward expressions of their love for God mean anything. David knew that it was not about "the system" but about "a relationship" with our God. Wow! Talk about a bold statement for a guy who broke two of the biggest rules in the religious rule book. This is the guy God chose as the forefather of an everlasting kingdom.

Case Study Three: Absalom is the perfect follow-up to a soft king like David. He is a leader for all the underdogs and outcasts. He is driven by a sense of justice. He stands up for all the victims in the world. People love this kind of rebel leader who sticks up for the little guy. Yet, his cry for justice is just a cover for his lust for power. His anger and ambition lead him to a mutinous rebellion and his own tragic death. Three down, but the best is yet to come.

Case Study Four: Solomon is the wisest king imaginable. He has everything going for him. Finally it looks like the kingdom will come together. Solomon makes sure all of God's rules are proclaimed to the people. He builds a gorgeous temple[1] for their rituals. So much for the humble tent God wanted. He shows himself to be a super-wise leader that protects the interests of the people and secures their borders to keep all the "bad" people away. Finally we will see everything as it should be. Right? Think again.

Solomon starts out well as king, having strong confidence in God, good intentions, and wisdom. But he begins using his wisdom to rationalize his actions. Motivated either by fear or ambition, he signs countless treaties with foreign nations so that he can secure his kingdom and preserve his legacy. He acquires massive wealth and military power, even though God had given strict warnings against doing this.

In the end, his failure to trust God for success leads him to turn to the gods and idols of the nations around Israel. He does not turn to God for security but relies on his own wisdom and turns to others.[2] The wisest king imaginable is self-deceived by his own wisdom. His greatest strength becomes his greatest weakness, and in the end, like many other kings before him, he fails.

In the end, what looked like Israel's final triumph, a dream come true, comes crashing to the ground along with the world's greatest leader. So much for following the examples of the nations around them. So much for great leadership turning everything around. So much for wisdom, riches, and power.

The problem with any leader we choose to put in charge is that they have the same issue everyone else has. Unless that person's heart is changed, the prestige and power that come with leadership will quickly corrupt even those with the best intentions.

Who are the leaders that I trust and follow?

How much hope do I put in these leaders to make my life all it can be?

7

Captivity

Act Three: Scene Four

THE SETS KEEP changing but the storyline continues down the same unfortunate path. Here in this final scene of the third act, we witness one king after another leading the people of Israel into idolatry and evil, with disastrous consequences. During this time, Israel is conquered by two successive powerful empires, Assyria and Babylon. Over the centuries, the Israelites are deported and taken into slavery by these empires. With the failure of Israel's kings, the focus of our story now shifts to a new kind of leader, one who leads in a different way from a king. This new kind of leader is called a prophet. Israel has had priests and kings, but these leaders are not making a difference. A prophet is simply someone God speaks through. God unleashes on Israel a series of prophets whose role is to shout out God's truth loud and clear, whether the people want to hear it or not.

Two particular prophets, Elijah and Elisha, emerge supercharged with divine power. They can command the elements of nature. They can stop it from raining, make rivers part, multiply food, and call fire to fall from heaven. They heal the sick and even raise the dead. Talk about special effects. You would think people would be running back to God like in the days of the parting of the Red Sea. Yet, none of these over-the-top miracles do anything to turn the people back to God.

Through these two prophets, God sends one severe punishment after another as a consequence for all the evil the people continue to commit. But none of this works to change their hearts. Their self-centered indulgence and self-saving obsessions leave them in complete depravity and isolation from God.

And so God sends prophet after prophet to warn the people and explain why they are being taken captive by these foreign empires. God is holding them accountable, and yet they cling to their worship of foreign gods that promise them wealth and prosperity. In their greed, they just cannot seem to stop their terrible treatment of the poor and vulnerable.

Amidst these stark warnings, the prophets of God make two bold and important announcements.

First, they communicate that God is eventually going to send a rescuer to save this family. The one who was promised back in the Garden of Eden is finally going to arrive and set the whole mess straight. One of these prophecies, spoken by the prophet Daniel, is filled with vivid imagery. It describes a great sea and four beasts coming out of the sea, the final one described as a horrifying horned dragon. It also depicts a rescuer called the "son of man," which really means "average guy,"[1] who comes with the powers of heaven and ultimately takes his seat in God's presence as the one who has ultimate authority. He is even worshipped. How can this be, since only God can be worshipped?

According to Daniel's vision this future "average guy" will establish an eternal kingdom on earth and give it over to those called Holy Ones.[2] The term "Holy Ones" was a title used for angelic messengers. Has Israel messed up so badly that it will take the armies of heaven to establish and defend God's kingdom on earth? Is this the only hope Israel has?

This first prophetic promise sets up the second great promise: when this rescuer comes, he will launch a new covenant between God and people.

> I was watching in the night visions, and with the clouds of the sky one like a son of man was approaching. He went up to the Ancient of Days and was escorted before him. To him was given ruling authority, honor, and sovereignty. All peoples, nations, and language groups were serving him. His authority is eternal and will not pass away. His kingdom will not be destroyed. . . . The holy ones of the Most High will receive the kingdom and will take possession of the kingdom forever and ever.
>
> DANIEL 7:13-14,18, NET

The old covenant, given through Moses to the Israelites, did not work, so a new one is needed. The big difference in the new covenant is that God will send his Spirit to change his people from the inside out.

The prophet Jeremiah describes the new covenant in detail. It clearly contrasts with the old covenant. Its focus is on transformation of hearts and minds. It will open the way for all people to know God. It will unleash God's forgiveness in a new, radical way.

A prophet named Ezekiel backs up Jeremiah and underscores that this inside-out heart transformation will come because God's Spirit will work inside of people. A prophet named Joel drives it home further by declaring that the promised work of the Spirit is for all people, young and old alike. This offer will be open to everyone.

These prophets leave no room for doubt. We all need a heart transplant, and the coming Savior will do what religion never could.

> "The days are coming," declares the LORD, "when I will make a new covenant with the people of Israel and with the people of Judah. It will not be like the covenant I made with their ancestors when I took them by the hand to lead them out of Egypt, because they broke my covenant, though I was a husband to them," declares the LORD.

"This is the covenant I will make with the people of Israel after that time," declares the LORD. "I will put my law in their minds and write it on their hearts. I will be their God, and they will be my people. No longer will they teach their neighbor, or say to one another, 'Know the LORD,' because they will all know me, from the least of them to the greatest," declares the LORD. "For I will forgive their wickedness and will remember their sins no more." [God speaking through Jeremiah.]

JEREMIAH 31:31-34

Then I will sprinkle clean water on you, and you will be clean. Your filth will be washed away, and you will no longer worship idols. And I will give you a new heart, and I will put a new spirit in you. I will take out your stony, stubborn heart and give you a tender, responsive heart. And I will put my Spirit in you so that you will follow my decrees and be careful to obey my regulations. [God speaking through Ezekiel.]

EZEKIEL 36:25-27, NLT

And afterward, I will pour out my Spirit on all people. Your sons and daughters will prophesy, your old men will dream dreams, your young men will see visions. Even on my servants, both men and women, I will pour out my Spirit in those days. [God speaking through Joel.]

JOEL 2:28-29

By the end of Act Three—this seemingly unending and grueling "story of what does not work"—we are left desperate. We just want to shout, "Get me away from these people." Yet, their story is a mirror. If we are honest, we see ourselves in this story all too clearly.

Having said all this, we find some amazing people in this third act. In one way, they are exceptional friends of God, and in another way still deeply flawed. People like Abram, Moses, David, and Elijah live as friends of God in a way that transcends the rules and rituals of religion. Yet none of these leaders fulfilled the promise of the one who would set all the wrongs right. None of them was the promised rescuer to come.

So where are we at the end of Act Three with this nation-sized family called Israel? The family that was rescued from slavery in Egypt now finds itself in a new form of slavery at the hands of foreigners. Many Israelites have been deported from their homeland and live as an oppressed people in other countries. Only a small remnant actually live in the Promised Land. Israel still has a rallying point for their worship of God but it is not a grand temple like the one Solomon built. That temple has been destroyed. During the time of the prophets they rebuilt a small, humble temple. In many ways, this new place of worship is closer to the simple tent that God originally asked for in the days of Israel's desert wanderings.

This part of Israel's story ends with a fizzle. We now enter a four hundred year intermission of complete silence from God's prophets. This is the ultimate exclamation point; from God's point of view, something has to change.

How easily do I reconsider my approach to life when everything goes wrong?

Or do I find myself digging in my heels even though nothing is working out the way I want?

As we look back over the four scenes of Act Three, what do we see? God selects the smallest, weakest, most unlikely family to use as a case study for the rest of the human race.

What do we tend to think will change our messed up lives and hearts?

"Give me the rules." God gave them all the rules they could ever have wanted.

"Give me my space." God gave them the Promised Land.

"Give me a strong leader to follow." God gave them kings.

"Hold me accountable when I screw up." God rewarded their successes and dished out consequences when they failed.

Did it work? Did this little family, humanity's case study, finally pull it together? Nope. It was nothing short of a complete disaster.

I think we all like to believe that, given the right environment, we will do the right thing. We are all good people, right? So the best way to transform our lives is to change ourselves from the outside in. Fix my environment. Get the right kind of influences around me. Remove the distractions and temptations. Then I will be the spectacularly wonderful human being I want to be, right?

The story of Israel painfully proves that, unfortunately, this approach simply does not work. Even the best religion—one given directly by God, that has all the right rules, offers a safe little cocoon like the Promised Land, has strong spiritual leaders like David and Solomon, and even dishes out the most severe, harsh accountability— will never change the human heart or fix our messed-up lives. Religion will never make us right on the inside or right with God. Talk about a shocker. As we journey through this third act, we see God demonstrate for all time and eternity that religion does not work.

As the curtain falls on the third act, the audience is left wondering what God, the author and main character of this story, will do next. How will he work a miracle to somehow redeem the struggling family that bears his name, this mess of a human race that fills the stage? How will he turn this nightmare into the dream he originally intended?

When I know I need to change, do I try to change myself from the outside in?

Do I try to change by using the approach, "Give me the rules, give me my space, give me strong leaders, and hold me accountable when I screw up"?

How has that worked for me?

Reflection on What Does Not Work

I listened as Alison explained to me how her addictions recovery group works. When they start off with a new group of people, she explained, the first thing they do is take out a huge whiteboard and have everyone in the group write down all the things they had tried to do in order to kick their addiction to alcohol. When they are done, the leader then says, "Tonight, can we all agree that none of this works?"

You see, before the leader can start to write out what actually does work to break the grip of addiction, everyone in that room has to grieve the fact that they do not know what works. They must realize that they cannot do it themselves, and that what ultimately does work is something that, at first, may not make any sense to them.

I cannot tell you how many times I have said to one of my kids, "Let me help you," only to hear them say (come on, say it with me), "I can do it." We are all the same. We could be on the verge of a nervous breakdown or even death itself, and yet we still dig in our heels and say, "I do not need help. I can fix this. I can do this." Our self-centeredness, reinforced by fear, locks us into a permanent addiction to trying to save ourselves. The only person I want to trust is me.

We all believe that we know what will work for us to change our own hearts. Yet, as we listen to the stories of Israel, it is like listening to an addict give an account of everything he or she tried and in the end did not work.

Let's walk through it together. Everyone on the planet starts out life believing basically the same thing: I will do the right thing if I am given the right environment. If I just have the right opportunity, I will be the kind of person I want to be.

Here is how that logic works. I am a good person. I want to do the right thing. If someone would just explain to me the right rules and principles and how it all works then I will know what to do. Now I know I can be tempted, so the other thing I need to do is get all those bad influences out of my life. Then sometimes my will gets a bit weak and I need someone to be there to push me in the right direction. I need a leader I can follow as a role model.

Oh, one more thing. I know I am going to screw up, so I definitely need a good swift kick in the butt to keep me on track. If I know I am going to suffer harsh consequences, then good, wholesome fear will keep me in line.

This describes the basic underpinnings of every world religion, every governmental system, and every self-improvement program. This principle is at the core: the way to change the human heart is from the outside in. Given the proper controls and a perfect environment, everyone will eventually do the right thing, yes? We are basically good people, right?

The story of Israel reveals over and over again that our efforts to control our external world may keep our bad behavior in check for a while, but it will not ultimately do anything to fundamentally change the drives and desires of the human heart. We are good because someone is there to enforce the rules. Once we are out from under the rules, away from the eyes of our leaders and free from harsh accountability, many of us simply seize the moment to do what we want, even though we know it is wrong. Just think about what happens during a natural disaster. As soon as the crisis makes law and order impossible to enforce, seemingly good people, even the most religious people, start to loot, rape, and pillage. What would you do if you knew you could get away with something and never be caught? It is a scary thought.

Through the story of Israel, God demonstrates that even the best religion, the one that he himself created, cannot fundamentally change the human heart and restore intimacy with God and others. We need something more. That was his point.

Yet we have to ask ourselves, was God going to abandon his people to perpetual failure? Was God going to do that because they did not live up to his standard of religious righteousness? Certainly not.

The human heart, with its drives and desires, must be changed from the inside out. Listen to what the later prophets of Israel declared as God's word to this messed up national family:

"I will put my law in their minds and write it on their hearts. I will be their God, and they will be my people" (Jeremiah 31:33).

"I will give them an undivided heart and put a new spirit in them; I will remove from them their heart of stone and give them a heart of flesh. Then they will follow my decrees and be careful to keep my laws. They will be my people, and I will be their God" (Ezekiel 11:19-20).

"I will give you a new heart and put a new spirit in you; I will remove from you your heart of stone and give you a heart of flesh. And I will put my Spirit in you and move you to follow my decrees and be careful to keep my laws. . . . You will be my people, and I will be your God" (Ezekiel 36:26-28).

"And afterward, I will pour out my Spirit on all people. Your sons and daughters will prophesy, your old men will dream dreams, your young men will see visions. Even on my servants, both men and women, I will pour out my Spirit in those days" (Joel 2:28-29).

Note that throughout Israel's story, prophecy, visions, and dreams were the basic way people would hear God speak to them personally.

Through the words of his prophets, God makes abundantly clear that the human heart does not need a better religion or another outside-in spiritual self-improvement program. We need God to do what he did for us in Act One: gather up the frail dust of our lives and breathe his Spirit into us, making us come alive. He needs to do a complete heart transplant by changing us from the inside out.

Once he does that, what can we expect? We can anticipate the same thing that our first parents experienced: the intimacy with our heavenly parent restored, in which he can talk to us and we can hang out with him. You see, God wants us to get back to the closeness we had in the garden. He wants that just as much as we want it. He wants to restore his dream. His love for us is that great.

Act Three ends with a renewed expectancy. We now know what does not work. We know what God wants to do to change us from the inside out. Now, the question is, "When will that rescuer come? When will the one promised to Adam and Eve appear to deal that final blow to evil and usher in this radically new way of living with God?"

8

Rescue

Act Four: Matthew to John

THE WAIT IS finally over. House lights dim. The audience waits in anticipation. All eyes are fixed on the stage, waiting for God, the author and main character, to again take center stage. Will he reveal how his dream for us will be turned into reality? Will he show us what actually does work to heal the human heart and restore us to intimate friendship with himself and others? Yes, the time has come to reveal the rescuer.

The feeling of anticipation could not be stronger. The prophets of Israel have been silent throughout a four hundred year intermission. Talk about a bathroom break.

As the curtain rises on Act Four, the plot really starts to pick up. We resume our story with Israel in captivity. This time she is not under the brutal rule of Egypt, Babylon, or Persia, but an enemy far worse: the Roman Empire.

The story of the long-awaited rescuer is the ultimate plot twist in this drama. His name is Jesus or Joshua, which literally means "God saves." He carries the same name as the military leader who first led Israel in conquest of the Promised Land. Will this be a repeat performance? Will he unite Israel in a violent revolt to restore freedom to their land? He has a plan but it is basically the exact opposite of everything the people of Israel expected.

His life starts out, not in a palace where kings are born, but rather in a place of obvious poverty, a simple stable where the poor keep their animals. He forms a new family, not from the sons of a marriage, but from twelve of the most unlikely guys you could imagine for such a rescue mission. Among these twelve, a few of them are even sworn enemies of each other. We have some fishermen, a tax collector who's on the payroll of the Roman Empire, a militant revolutionary who hates the Romans and their tax collectors, and a bunch of other nobodies. Talk about a motley crew.

The new community that forms around Jesus is inclusive. Both men and women learn together. Rich and poor sit side by side. Prostitutes, drunkards, and swindlers are freely given a second chance at life. He keeps telling everyone that he is the "son of man," that "average guy" prophesied by Daniel. He proclaims that God's kingdom is coming but declares that it is not of this world. It is a kingdom without borders or hierarchy or sword. The battle Jesus wages is against spiritual forces, not Roman soldiers.

Over and over again, Jesus confronts and casts out the demons that lurk in the shadows of the human heart and secretly oppress people. His miracles outdo the great works of Elijah.[1] But his miracles come with a punch line. Again and again, Jesus breaks religious law and then performs a miracle to show that he has the authority to do what only God could do.

In all of this, neither his message nor his actions line up with what you expect of a good religious leader. He consistently does the opposite of everything the religious leaders thought God wanted. How could this man who trashes religion be the long expected rescuer from God? Well, it is time to find out. Here is a brief summary of what Jesus teaches.

Should the Law and religious rules control our lives? No. Love must be our guide. Jesus summarizes the entire Law with two simple commands. First, love God with everything you are and have and second, love your neighbor as you would love yourself. In Jesus' famous

Sermon on the Mount, he takes the idea of loving others beyond anything anyone had heard before. God wants us to love even our enemies.

This leads right into a second radical teaching. Should the security of the Promised Land be top priority and all enemies driven out? No. Jesus calls us to get close to our enemies and show them love, because they are just like us and God is at work in their hearts too.

Jesus illustrates this idea powerfully through his interaction with a Roman centurion, the captain of one hundred enemy Roman soldiers. This centurion needs a miracle to save his daughter from imminent death, and he sees that Jesus is his only hope. Jesus is glad to respond to this man's trust in God and heals his daughter. Jesus then makes a bold statement: this enemy Roman soldier has more genuine faith than any Israelite. What? How could he say that a pagan trusts God more than all the Israelites who have been schooled in the Law? The answer is simple. God looks at the heart.

I can picture the religious leaders of Jesus' day protesting: "But these are all pagan sinners." Jesus does not stop there. He is on a roll. Should the temple and all of its prescribed rituals be their source of getting right with God? Jesus shocks his hearers again. No. They do not need the temple any longer because God's rescuer has arrived and is dishing out God's forgiveness, free of charge.

On a regular basis throughout his ministry, Jesus forgives people directly. No sacrifices or trips to the temple are needed. Only God can forgive sins, right? Jesus answers this question directly. In one account, Jesus meets a paralyzed man in Capernaum. Jesus forgives the man's sins, and immediately the religious leaders freak out. Only God can forgive sins, right? Jesus must be blaspheming. Jesus responds to their challenge by physically healing the man. As the paralyzed man gets up, picks up his mat, and walks home, the jaws of the religious skeptics drop to the ground at both his audacity and power. Jesus' willingness to freely distribute forgiveness sets the stage for a final surprising teaching.

We should all fear harsh accountability and dire consequences if we screw up, right? Nope. Harsh accountability is not what we need. What we need is lavish grace: a divine love and forgiveness freely given to us, especially when we screw up.

Okay, here is one more story. A woman is caught in adultery. The Law says she should be put to death by stoning. A zealous religious crowd drags her before Jesus to see what he, as a good religious teacher, would say. He has to only make one simple statement to disarm them all: "Let the person without sin be the first one to throw a stone." All we hear is silence. Then, one at a time, the rocks that the men clutched begin to fall to the ground as the defeated crowd disperses.

As Jesus and the woman are left standing alone in the street staring at one another, what does Jesus do with this guilty woman? No judgment. He simply forgives her and calls her to start on a new path. He makes it so easy.

Surprisingly, Jesus ends up doing the exact opposite of what any good religious person would expect. He forgives rather than condemns. He does not help people follow religion. He offers a completely different way to God.

Do I find myself agreeing or disagreeing with Jesus' key teachings? Why do they resonate, or not resonate, with my experience?

[A teaching from Jesus on God's desire for love, rather than religious law:]

One of them, an expert in religious law, tried to trap him with this question: "Teacher, which is the most important commandment in the law of Moses?"

Jesus replied, "'You must love the LORD your God with all your heart, all your soul, and all your mind.' This is the first and greatest commandment. A second is equally important: 'Love your neighbor as yourself.' The entire law and all the demands of the prophets are based on these two commandments."

MATTHEW 22:35-40, NLT

[A story from Jesus' life where he shows how we all need loving forgiveness, not the harsh judgment of religious law·]

Jesus returned to the Mount of Olives, but early the next morning he was back again at the Temple. A crowd soon gathered, and he sat down and taught them. As he was speaking, the teachers of religious law and the Pharisees brought a woman who had been caught in the act of adultery. They put her in front of the crowd.

"Teacher," they said to Jesus, "this woman was caught in the act of adultery. The law of Moses says to stone her. What do you say?"

They were trying to trap him into saying something they could use against him, but Jesus stooped down and wrote in the dust with his finger. They kept demanding an answer, so he stood up again and said, "All right, but let the one who has never sinned throw the first stone!" Then he stooped down again and wrote in the dust.

When the accusers heard this, they slipped away one by one, beginning with the oldest, until only Jesus was left in the middle of the crowd with the woman. Then Jesus stood up again and said to the woman, "Where are your accusers? Didn't even one of them condemn you?"

"No, Lord," she said.

And Jesus said, "Neither do I. Go and sin no more."

JOHN 8:1-11, NLT

Jesus was fond of telling stories to drive home his points. One day, he tells the religious leaders a story that summarizes his message in a way that really hits home, a story about a gracious father and two sons who had some issues. The story points out that there are two basic problems with the human heart and demonstrates that God is a loving Father who desires to rescue and restore us. Let me summarize.

The story opens with a younger brother who demands his inheritance from his dad before his father has even died. Talk about hurtful and insulting. He then spends every good thing he receives on his own indulgence—partying, prostitutes, the works. To no one's surprise, he ends up bankrupt in a pigsty eating pig food. Disgusting! Finally, after coming to his senses, he humbly returns to his father, completely broken with the realization that he has screwed up his entire life. His highest hope is that his father will take him back into his household, not as a son, but as a servant.

When the son approaches the father, does his father freak out and kick him out of the family for his shameful failure? No, his father loves him completely and offers the most wildly lavish grace and forgiveness to him. In fact, his partying son soon discovers that the best party in the world is right in his father's house. Yes, his father holds a massive celebration for his long-lost child.

So what do we learn from the younger brother's story? We learn that a major problem with the human heart is that it is fundamentally self-centered, which leads to perpetual self-indulgence. We love to spend every good thing that God gives us on ourselves.

But this problem comes with a measure of hope. Relentless self-indulgence will ultimately wreck our lives and relationships. In the end, it will produce such painful consequences that we have the hope of coming to our senses and realizing that perpetual self-indulgence is a dead end. We actually may reach back out to God for help, even if we find ourselves in a divorce court, a bankruptcy office, a prison cell, or on our death bed.

And what do we discover when we reach out to God? We learn that God loves us more than we can imagine and he can meet our needs better than we can for ourselves. What incredible news for all of us who struggle with self-indulgence. What a happy ending.

But there is another son and another ending. His story is not so much intended for messed-up people as it is for religious people. It reveals a second major problem with the human heart, another manifestation of self-centeredness. It can easily feel proudly superior to others. It can think it has done everything right, at least according to its own standards. This is the story of the older brother.

When the younger brother returns home after ruining his life, his brother is furious. He self-righteously judges his brother and completely rejects him. He is also indignant because his father has thrown an expensive party for his failure of a brother. He refuses to attend the party.

But the father reaches out to him. He pleads with him to stop working out in field and join the party. He begs him to let go of his judgmental self-righteousness and join the celebration of grace and restored relationship.

So does the older brother let go of his self-righteousness and bitterness and join the party? We never find out. Jesus leaves his listeners hanging. But Jesus has a point in stopping the story where he does. Remember who is in his audience? It was the religious leaders who were ticked off at Jesus for showing so much grace to people who had messed up. Jesus has led his audience, and all of us, to this question: will we join God's party, where everyone gets to experience his amazing love and forgiveness?

The story of the older brother reveals a difficult problem with the human heart: the tendency to be self-righteous and judgmental toward those who screw up. Both are forms of self-centeredness that can creep into our thinking unnoticed.

The younger brother had moral sin issues; the older brother had religious sin issues. The older brother was just as far away from his father relationally as his younger brother was. Instead of living in the brothel of self-indulgence as his brother did, he dwelled in the fields of his own self-righteousness. He may have been physically close to home, but in his heart he too was in a far-off land of entitlement, self-righteousness, and the bitter judgment of others.

In some ways, the older brother's "heart condition" was worse than his younger brother's. Because it did not deliver the same kind of painful consequences into his life that the younger brother experienced, he never got to that broken place. Like him, we too can be addicted to our own religiosity, never feeling broken and humbled, and potentially going our entire lives without ever coming to our senses.

Perhaps this explains why the religious leaders, for the most part, did not respond to Jesus' message while many of the "sinners" did. The message of grace and forgiveness apart from religion requires us to repent, not just from all the sins that we hate but from the sins we love — our religious sins. We must give up our addiction to hiding our true selves behind the bushes of religion. We must give up our tendency to judge and condemn anyone who does not measure up.

The story of the older brother ends with the father begging his son to leave his religious self-righteousness and to join the party of forgiveness and grace. Imagine a God so humble as to plead with that religious judgmental part of the older brother's heart, and of our hearts too, to call us out of self-righteousness and into a life of radical grace and restored friendships.

Do I identify more with the self-indulgent younger son or the judgmental older son?

What gave Jesus the right to challenge the religious leaders? Who does he think he is to go up against the entire religious establishment? In a simple statement, Jesus provides the answer: "I and the Father are one."[2] Over and over Jesus did and said things that were unthinkable for a Jew of his day. He declared by his actions that he was "God with us."

By what he said and did, Jesus revealed that God himself had now come to planet earth to declare that the time was at hand to deal that final blow to evil. This included, as shocking as it seemed, human religion as a source of that evil.

As we now move forward in the rescuer's story, we are going to see an Old-West style showdown occur. It is time for God, through his chosen high plains drifter, to set the slaves of self-centeredness free.

Does Jesus march into the Roman ruler's palace to take on an oppressive political enemy, as Moses did of Pharaoh? No. Jesus enters the temple in Jerusalem to take on the religious establishment. One of the first things he does there is to start driving out all the people who were buying and selling things, including those who were selling doves to people who wanted to make a sacrifice. He also turned over the tables of the money changers, who had set themselves up as small-time bankers. Jesus effectively shuts down the sacrificial system for a day and clears the way for people to draw near to God.

Jesus is making a bold statement: God is not interested in wiping out our enemies but in wiping out a religious approach to life that makes it hard for people, including enemies, to get close to God.

It does not take a genius to guess what happens next. Jesus' act of religious subversion at the temple is the final straw. The religious leaders would have seen it as the ultimate insult to their authority and their way of life. So they set their scopes on Jesus. They want to protect their positions of power and privilege. It is now just a matter of time before they take this irreligious revolutionary out.

The occasion is Passover, the great annual celebration of Israel's rescue from Egypt. On this night, all the people of Israel gather in homes to share a meal and celebrate their historic and miraculous deliverance from Egypt. That day, Jesus meets with his twelve disciples to share the Passover meal with them. But another deliverance is about to take place.

At the meal, Jesus makes a series of startling announcements. First, he tells them that one of the twelve will betray him, leading to his death. Horrified, the disciples look around the room and ask themselves, "Who will it be?" Jesus then asks them to remember this historic night in the future by sharing bread and wine together. The bread would represent his broken body, the wine the blood he would shed for them. Even with these symbols Jesus makes an irreligious choice. The Law forbade the drinking of blood, and yet he commands his disciples to symbolically drink his blood and eat his broken body.

But wait. There is more. His final announcement is the clincher. He tells them that the new covenant the prophets foretold begins now. Soon, God will send his Spirit to change people, not from the outside in, through religious rules and systems, but from the inside out.

After the meal, Jesus retreats to a garden to pray to his Father. He is full of emotional torment as he stares down the barrel of his impending fate. As predicted, that night Judas, his own disciple, leads a group of soldiers directly to Jesus in the garden and betrays him with a kiss.

Jesus is now in custody.

The religious leaders pull the necessary political levers.

He is tried as a criminal and brutally beaten.

He is given a crown of thorns and a robe and mocked as the king of the Jews.

He is publically executed on a Roman cross as a heretical revolutionary.

How in the world could Jesus be the long-awaited rescuer of humanity if he died, and died in such humiliating agony and defeat? How could his message be true? How could he be God's promised one?

Jesus' followers figured that this was the end of the story. But they were mistaken. Jesus' Father had other plans. As Jesus predicted, three days after his death the miracle that changed the course of human history occurs. Jesus is resurrected to life. The first to see him are his closest female disciples. Then Peter and the other disciples see him. And then up to five hundred people see Jesus resurrected and alive.[3] What in the world could this mean? What could God be doing in this dramatic and mind-blowing demonstration of his power?

Act Four ends with Jesus' small band of followers struggling to understand all of this. They are confused and trying to figure out what in the world just happened. Everything they knew has been flipped on its head.

Jesus is not dead, but alive.

This is not the end but a new beginning.

All hope is not lost.

The dream is alive.

If Jesus was truly raised to life by God, what would that mean for my life?

Reflection on Rescue

Some things seem too good to be true. I remember the day my sister and I realized we held in our hands a winning lottery ticket. I was ten years old, and my sister was twelve.

Someone had given my dad a lottery ticket. He thought it was worthless and was going to throw it in the garbage. My sister and I thought we should see if it was a winner. We took the ticket, checked the numbers, and yep, we had won—brace yourself—one thousand dollars! I remember thinking, We are insanely rich.

That happened many years ago, and I now have a better perspective. Yet, I can appreciate the complete shock, confusion, and wonder that the followers of Jesus must have felt as they processed his life, death, and resurrection. They must have felt like they had won the eternal billion-dollar lottery. Everyone can be immediately restored to a full relationship with God without the requirements of religion. Life after death is now tangibly validated because of Jesus' resurrection. Is it too good to be true? Or is it so good it must be God? Let's take a closer look at the central messages of Jesus' life and teaching. For convenience, I will break it down to four of his most basic messages.

First, Jesus exposes the inadequacy of a religious, rules-oriented approach to life and then declares that it must be replaced by the love ethic that deals with people on a case-by-case basis.[4] A religious, rules-oriented approach to life comes from our desire to manage our environments and fix ourselves from the outside in. We want to codify what is right and wrong, making everything binary—black or white, yes or no. Once we have figured out the rules, then we can determine how we are doing, and even better, we can figure out how everyone else is doing. It is incredibly soothing to our souls to get a list of rules that we are comfortable with. It enables us to continuously remind ourselves that we are doing okay, because we can more easily get our own spiritual A grade (at least according to our own rules) and be (again according to our own rules) a notch above many others.

Jesus' "love ethic" teaches that love must determine the right thing in each situation. It invites us to take time to learn how to empathize with others, to look at life through their eyes.

It calls us to be compassionate, not judgmental.

It leads us out of a self-righteous, self-saving addiction into a relational approach to loving others.

It calls us to adapt to and to meet other people's needs with a case-by-case approach.

And, by the way, this is much harder work than following a set of rules that are set in stone. The love ethic of Jesus, for instance, sits in stark contrast to the rule-based way, which is so easily manipulated. If I am honest with myself, I have to admit that I can manipulate a list of rules in my favor. I can decide which rules are going to be important to me. I can create my own justifications for the exceptions I allow. And I can devise a rationale for why someone who fails me does not deserve my mercy. In the end I get what I want, but only according to my rules. The actions of the hypocrites of Jesus' day showed how easy this was to do.

Second, Jesus taught his followers to love their enemies.[5] He was explicit: love your enemies, do good to those who persecute you, turn the other cheek. We should not just "not do to others what we do not want them to do to us."[6] This passive approach — "you leave me alone and I will leave you alone" — is not enough. Jesus taught a proactive, go on the offensive, disarm your enemy with kindness, approach. Think of it as "eliminating your enemies by converting them into your friends." In the end you may not make everyone a friend. And that is okay, because not everyone needs to be a friend. But you will certainly have ended a cycle of anger, resentment, and even hatred.

This may sound ridiculous, even dangerous, but through his enemy-love teaching, Jesus gets at the very core of our destructive self-centeredness and fear. Our anger dehumanizes people when we vilify them. In reality, we need to remember that they are not much different than we are. They are worthy of love, and God is at work in their lives too.

As we consider Jesus' teaching, we can see how it fundamentally changes our whole approach to life. His approach is to create a safe world through reconciled relationships rather than simply banking on power and might. He does not promote the security and safety of a Promised Land or country with a well-defended border; he proclaims the power of an open border. We are to be a community where love disarms hate and we are secure because we sacrificially live as peacemakers in a world of hostility and distrust.

Jesus calls us out of our own obsession with comfort, defense, and survival into the higher calling of laying down our lives so that others may live. Jesus led the way in demonstrating the power of loving one's enemies by willingly dying for them.

Now he calls us to go and do likewise.

Third, Jesus, in what he said and did, called people to step free of social hierarchies and enter into an inclusive community. Jesus' life and teaching cast a vision of a family under a heavenly Father where the strongest serve the weakest, the richest serve the poorest, and the oldest serve the youngest.[7] In this community, there are no human kings or captains or chiefs. There is only one King, one commander and chief, and he is the ultimate servant. There are no special titles, prideful posturing, or popularity contests. There is no clutching and clawing to climb the leadership ladder.

We must embrace the truth that we are all equally valued. We are all brothers and sisters. There is no pecking order, no elite class, and no religious caste system. It is a family what God, our Divine Parent, wants above all else.

The last important idea that Jesus taught was that radical grace, a freely offered forgiveness and love, needs to be lavishly given to everyone who has messed up, and given without adding harsh consequences.[8] This is another of those counterintuitive principles that Jesus teaches. And today it may seem particularly odd, given our revenge-oriented world. But as we have seen, the harsh consequences that descended on Israel because of its disobedience — death, disease, war, and destruction — did nothing in the long run to restrain the people's self-destructive impulses. The Old Testament is one long, sad history of that fact.

Instinctively, we may feel that if people are not held accountable by harsh consequences they will go crazy and get lost in self-indulgence. But that is not necessarily so. Jesus looks for a higher motivation in those he loves. He knows there is a better way for people to live.

Jesus' approach is simple. He knows that the sweetness of a generous love trains the heart toward loyal devotion of what is right and good in a way that judgment and punishment never could. Fear only keeps us in line when someone has a stick raised over our heads. On the other hand, when we experience a generous love, it can so secure our hearts that we want to be loyal to that person in response. Why? Because we do not want to let down the person who loves us so much. Our hearts want to return that love by faithfully loving and being loyal to the person.

You see, when God's perfect love has driven out our fear, we experience a deep sense of belonging, safety, and peace; that profound sense of love then empowers us to make relationship-honoring decisions. If we mess up, we can confidently return to the security of that love to get back on our feet and be restored to full relationship.

Love, not fear, has the only power to truly change the human heart. Now I know, in many ways, this idea seems counterintuitive. Yet it is exactly what we need and what, deep down, many of us want.

As we continue to stare into the life of our rescuer, there is one more profound revelation we must consider. It comes, not only out of how he lived or what he taught, but also out of the way he died, and then what happened after he died. I think it is easy to understand why the disciples, at first, did not believe Jesus had risen from the dead. I think it is also easy to understand why, once they did believe it, they did not have a sweet clue what to do with that information. A miracle of this proportion overloads human circuitry.

What is the meaning of Jesus' death and resurrection? The first disciples finally come to understand the following ramifications.[9]

Jesus' followers come to see that Jesus, in a very real way, was "God with us." As they reflected on his death and resurrection, they began to grasp the profound mystery that, through Jesus, God had come and done what only God could do. In his sacrificial death, Jesus somehow became the final sacrifice for all that is wrong in this world.[10] Jesus selflessly triumphed over all self-centeredness, sin, religion, evil, and even death itself. He willingly became the one sacrifice that meant that no other religious sacrifices would ever be necessary. For millennia, world religions portrayed the gods as angry, vindictive deities demanding bloody sacrifices before they would forgive or bless humans. The sacrificial system within Israel had a different message. Yes, breaking covenant brings death, but God had given this system out of his desire to forgive and restore relationship. The first disciples realized that God had entered right into our own religious mind-set and, through Jesus, became the final sacrifice. There was nothing left for us to do to make ourselves right before God. God himself had done everything from start to finish. Religion, even the religion God himself instituted, was now obsolete. Whatever value religion offered humanity was no longer needed. A new way was now open for people to be intimate friends with God.

They also realized that death had been defeated. Just as one act by the first man and woman had set in motion everything that went wrong and led to our death, through Jesus God with one act was reversing this. There is life after death, and Jesus opened the door to that eternal existence. We do not have to be afraid of dying. We are now free to live the way God intended.

Lastly, they came to see that through Jesus God unleashed a new order and a new way of doing things. Jesus called it a new kingdom, a kingdom that transcends and will outlast all other kingdoms.

This kingdom would restore his vision for a global family where people live and love as he intended.

As he promised, God sent a rescuer, one who dealt that final, decisive blow to evil, even at the cost of his own life. Who would have thought God himself would be that rescuer?

Community

Act Five: Acts to Revelation

Scene One

THE AUDIENCE SHIFTS in their seats with nervous excitement. As the curtains rise and Act Five opens, they wonder, how will God use this small, unlikely group of nobodies to change the world? Is God's grace, love, and power capable of turning such average people into world-changing, irreligious revolutionaries?

Our story continues as Jesus miraculously ascends to heaven. The resurrected King returns victorious and is now seated at the right hand of God his Father.[1] Before leaving, however, Jesus commands his disciples to wait together until God's Spirit comes and launches them into their new mission, transforming their hearts and lives. Things are about to go into overdrive.

So they gather together to pray in Jerusalem, the center of their world as they know it, during a special Jewish celebration. They are brimming with anticipation for what God is going to do next through them. They do not have to wait long. The Spirit of God comes on their lives. They see what looks like fire resting on them, just like when God's presence filled the tabernacle or temple. God's power and presence is in them and ready to launch them into their new mission. They feel joy. They feel loved to the core. They feel ready to take on the world. It causes them to party like they have never partied before. There is food, friendship, singing, laughter, and generous sharing with anyone in need.[2]

It gets better. The inner transformation of this seemingly defeated group is now accompanied by a powerful miraculous sign for all to see. To the amazement of the entire city of Jerusalem, these Christ-followers spontaneously and boldly speak in different kinds of languages, which they would not normally be able to do. The city is filled with international Jews who are attending the festivities, and the message of Christ is amazingly proclaimed to these people in their native languages. It was bizarre and unforgettable.

With this powerful outpouring of his Spirit, God basically reverses a miracle that he did long ago at the Tower of Babel. Remember in Act Three, Scene One and the building project that went sideways? Now, in Jerusalem, suddenly everyone understands what is being said. What a perfect kickoff for a global family movement. Everyone, no matter what race, status, gender, or nationality, can be set right with God. What a great way to welcome all nations into a new community with God.

Peter replied, "Each of you must repent of your sins and turn to God, and be baptized in the name of Jesus Christ for the forgiveness of your sins. Then you will receive the gift of the Holy Spirit. This promise is to you, and to your children, and even to the Gentiles — all who have been called by the Lord our God." Then Peter continued preaching for a long time, strongly urging all his listeners, "Save yourselves from this crooked generation!"

Those who believed what Peter said were baptized and added to the church that day — about 3,000 in all.

ACTS 2:38-41, NLT

All the believers devoted themselves to the apostles' teaching, and to fellowship, and to sharing in meals (including the Lord's Supper), and to prayer.

A deep sense of awe came over them all, and the apostles performed many miraculous signs and wonders. And all the believers met together in one place and shared everything they had. They sold their property and possessions and shared the money with those in need. They worshiped together at the Temple each day, met in homes for the Lord's Supper, and shared their meals with great joy and generosity — all the while praising God and enjoying the goodwill of all the people. And each day the Lord added to their fellowship those who were being saved.

Acts 2:42-47, NLT

Not everyone is thrilled with this rapidly growing movement. Can you guess who is ticked off? The religious leaders are obviously threatened and launch an investigation into what the stir is all about. It does not take long before their inquiry ignites their wrath. They kill a Christ-follower named Stephen and launch a full-scale persecution. Will persecution quickly snuff out this new movement? Once again the Divine Author delivers up plot twist after plot twist to get our attention. Once again God does the unexpected. Brace yourself.

The persecution against the Christ-followers is intense and at the center of it is a very intense guy. His name is Saul of Tarsus, and he is one of the most religious guys in Israel, a violent, hyper-legalist who is ambitious and relentless in his religious zeal.[3] He is hell-bent on wiping out the Christ-followers, who dare to threaten his precious religious system with their message. Remember the story Jesus told about the father and his two sons we talked about earlier? Well, Saul was much like the older brother in the story, the one who followed the rules and hated all the talk of forgiveness and grace.

In a stunning turn of events, Saul, this archenemy of Jesus' message, gets a personal, supernatural appearance from none other than the resurrected Jesus himself. He ends up receiving more grace than he could handle. In fact, he ironically receives so much grace that he is now transformed into a one-man religion-wrecking machine and becomes a key leader of the early Jesus movement. He begins to preach the very message he once railed against. He now loves those who were previously his enemies. He even takes on a new name, Paul, to show everyone how much he has been transformed.

We see in the conversion of Saul what loving your enemy really looks like. Jesus, even after his resurrection, shows the early Christ-followers and all of us who read the story, that only love has the power to make enemies into allies.

Most of the writings that we have today from the first-century church come from the life and teachings of Paul, a true irreligious revolutionary. They chronicle how he and his companions take on the entire religious establishment in the name of Jesus. Every form of religion gets targeted by this revolution, whether legalistic, ritualistic, magical, philosophical, or political. All rulers, governors, and kings, and even Caesar himself, get officially put on notice that there is a new kingdom coming to town. It is a revolution that will call humanity back from the exile of religion to a home built around a loving, unified community. It is a global family led by our one true Divine Parent.

Do I think the world needs this kind of revolution, this kind of community?

Do I want to be a part of this kind of movement?

As we read through the Epistles, the writings of this first band of Christ-followers, what do we find? Did they live in utopia? No. Far from it. Radical grace, inclusive community, and an irreligious approach to God and life do not remove all human struggles. Instead, as we saw in our earlier stories, these writings provide a new way to approach our problems. As we experience God's love in our lives, we can then have the courage to extend his love and forgiveness to others in the midst of our real-life problems and struggles.

The writings of leaders like Paul, Peter, and John provide great insights into the struggles, failures, and successes of the first Christ-followers. They help us see that a new way of living is absolutely possible. These writers often referred to the followers of Christ as "holy ones,"[4] a name taken from the prophecy in the book of Daniel. This term implies that they are set apart for a special purpose. Through God's Spirit at work in their lives and relationships, they are being restored to wholeness and commissioned for a special purpose in the world: to become God's messengers of help, healing, and reconciliation to all people. As Daniel prophesied long ago, these "holy ones" help bring God's kingdom to earth.

Within this first generation, the movement slowly spreads across the Roman Empire. People gather in homes on a weekly basis to share life as family. They rally together in public settings, in rented halls, and even in religious gathering places. They invite everyone, including spiritual seekers and religious adherents, to hear the incredible news about an irreligious way to live as a friend of God. It is no surprise that they suffer severe persecution. As more and more people see the love and join the movement, the religious and political establishments soon sense the threat of this new kingdom.

The Roman Empire had established its own version of peace, called the "Pax Romana," or Roman Peace. It brought peace by crushing kingdoms and forcing people to bow down to its emperor-god. It is not hard to see how talk of a new kingdom whose highest allegiance is to God got the attention of local rulers and governors.

In all of this, the Christ-followers remained steadfast in their conviction, despite being reviled, tortured, and even put to death at times. They served a risen King. They carried the message of hope for the planet. They found new equality among themselves, one not based on gender, race, or social status. They awaited the return of their King, when all things will be restored. The power of God's Spirit was in them and nothing could stop them. They had an undying love for

God and for all people, and so they wanted everyone and anyone to hear the message.

As we come to the close of this scene, the vision of an ever growing movement is alive and well. Triumph is right around the corner, right? What could prevent such a vibrant, passionate community from spreading across the world and transforming it with Jesus' vision of peace and restoration? What could stop a people so compelled by God's dream? What could possibly go wrong? Well, as we all know, old habits die hard.

For what truth or mission would I be willing to suffer or die?

10

Christendom

Act Five: AD 100 to the Present Time

Scene Two

AS WE MOVE into the second scene of the fifth act the stage is notably darker. This part of the story continues past the pages of the Bible into the pages of the history books that succeed it. Although the stories about the Christian church recorded by historians have often been treated by the church as "deleted scenes," they are vital to understanding our present context (or should I say, our mess).

For almost three hundred years after the resurrection of Christ, the underground, religiously subversive revolution of Jesus continues to advance and penetrate virtually every strata of the Roman Empire. This new community places a high value on all people, regardless of age, sex, race, or status, including children, women, and slaves. They model compassion to the poor and sick in a way that is foreign to the Roman culture of the day. They demonstrate a kind of self-control that contrasts some of the excesses of their time, such as public violence, orgies, and gluttonous feasts. They courageously face severe persecution, with many of the community dying as martyrs.

Yet they are far from a perfect community. In-house debates strain their sense of community and unity. Competitive teaching movements attract followers to leave the love ethic of Jesus. Persecution threatens the lives of their best leaders. But nothing can stop this compassionate, family-styled, deeply devoted community. They invite more and more people to join their movement, to embrace Jesus as the rescuing King.

Brace yourself for another massive plot twist.

What could stop this underground movement? Remember the old saying, "If you can't beat them, join them"? By AD 312, Christianity has settled into the mainstream, and some would say too nicely. In a pivotal moment, Constantine, Emperor of Rome, decides to make Christianity the state religion in an effort to unite a fragmenting empire. He makes this decision after reportedly seeing a vision of the cross before a battle and finding inspiration for a military victory. Ironically, the sign of the cross, which for Jesus' followers was the symbol of self-sacrifice for their peace-focused movement, now becomes the standard on shields and flags of the Roman political and military kingdom.

How in the world could this happen after centuries of persecution? How could the cross so quickly become a symbol of warfare after having been carried by the Prince of Peace to his death? There are many theories of why Constantine aligned himself with Christianity, but the fact remains that God's underground radical movement is now hijacked to support a new state-blessed religion that is in opposition to what Jesus intended for his kingdom.

The Romans now begin converting pagan temples into churches and creating a hierarchy of priests. Within just one generation, the revolution bent on opposing religion, the movement that teaches a relational connection to God, becomes one of the most massive and structured religions in history. Is this ironic or what?

Tack on the conversion of the great Platonist philosopher Augustine, who rationally works out all the details of why Christianity makes sense for a great state religion, and presto! Everything is flipped on its head again, save for a remnant of faithful people through the centuries who steward Jesus' original vision. The movement Jesus initiated gets taken over by a hierarchical, oppressive, legalistic, and violent religion.

Could this have been the counter-maneuver of that ancient enemy Satan?

Throughout the centuries, from approximately AD 300–1500, there is a real confusing mix of Jesus-inspired acts of love and religiously inspired atrocities arising from those who call themselves Christian.

On the one hand, faithful Christ-followers are doing their best to live out Jesus-teaching, often in very humble circumstances and slipping through life unnoticed. Many of these servants of God live in monasteries, insulated from the larger political arena. Elsewhere, women and men work together to serve the poor, live in community, preserve the writings of the first Christ-followers, and grow in intimate friendship with God. But these glowing examples of Jesus' love ethic are more the exception than the rule in the mainstream.

On the other hand, overshadowing the faithful, we have the institutional church constantly entangling itself in political ambition and ruthless oppression. The religion that claims to follow Jesus becomes one of the most destructive forces on the planet. Church leaders call Christians to embark on crusades to slaughter people in the name of a holy war and advance the kingdom of God on earth through force. They hunt and execute alleged heretics under the guise of protecting the faithful. They use torturous Inquisitions and witch hunts to root out evil from the community. They launch national wars under the banner of advancing the church of God. And all of this is done in Jesus' name.

It is as if many Christian religious leaders are trying to reenact the story of Israel. Although they venerate the Bible within the walls of cathedrals and churches, it is clear from the historical record that few really understood its message of Jesus' love ethic.[1] The institutional church, with its religious tradition and theology, in most ways lived in contradiction to the story of God.

Is my perception of God more shaped by Jesus or by the failures of the Christian church?

But then a slow process of rediscovery begins.

Around four hundred years ago, average people begin to read the story of Jesus themselves in the Bible. The invention of the printing press and the translation of the Bible into the common language open the way for average people to encounter this forgotten story, where before, they had to rely on professional holy men to tell them what God wanted of them.

Bit by bit those who are curious about Jesus and what he originally taught begin to see that their view of God just does not line up with Jesus' message. People begin to see that a lot has to change if they are going to get back to the original vision of Jesus and his message of hope.

Despite these advances, as centuries pass the church ends up focusing on only a portion of what Jesus taught. Much of the church emphasizes God's desire to rescue people from moral sin, but it neglects the more deceptive trap of the destructive addiction to religious pride.

The church warns sinners about hell, but it fails to warn Christians about religious sin with its hypocrisy and hard-hearted legalism. There is little mention of the sin that motivated the religious leaders of Jesus' time to reject him. Remember Jesus' story of the father and his two sons? It is as if the church during this period believes that the biggest problem facing humanity is the "younger brother" part of our hearts. They miss the point that perhaps the church itself is acting like the older brother in its stubborn addiction to religious, legalistic sin. Once again we see how insidious this blind spot can be.

Sadly, to this day, the full meaning of God's story remains lost for many who want to follow Jesus. Many sincere people still live in the cold grip of religion. Countless people are frantically trying to change their hearts by doing what does not work. They are crying out inside like the people of Israel did so many times before: "Give me the rules, give me my space (with no bad people around), give me a strong leader, and hold me accountable."

This effort expresses itself in the different kinds of churches people attend. Some are drawn to authoritative or ultra-conservative churches. Others move toward more liberal-minded, yet traditional churches.

Others gather in highly experiential, charismatic churches. And still others find their primary meaning in politics, in the hope of making their nation into a fully Christian country. The common theme behind all of these approaches is people trying to change themselves and others from the outside in.

But something is starting to rumble again, the whispers of revolution.

Will God's family rise up once again to tell the great story of God's love and explain what it means? Will they cast aside their lists of rules and embrace the radical love ethic of Jesus? Will they abandon their cocooned communities to engage a needy world? Will they become brothers and sisters again who serve everyone and welcome anyone? Will they lay aside all the ways they dish out harsh consequences to those who fail and allow God's divine presence to flood their lives and relationships with radical grace, mercy, and love?

God's dream for humanity has always been with us. Many of us simply live oblivious to it. You see, unless we grasp God's story and can see with fresh eyes that grand narrative of history, how will we discover where we can weave our own story into that unfolding drama? How will we begin to improvise its truths and themes? How will we be able to join in this life-changing adventure?

There are other scenes still to be written.

What would happen if Christians today started to live this inside out approach to God and relationships?

How would my life change if I decided to follow Jesus and this way of relating to God and others?

Reflection on Community and Christendom

Have you ever had this experience? Maybe you are on vacation or visiting distant friends. You drive through a strange town, leaning over your steering wheel, eyes scanning the unfamiliar surroundings to see if you missed your turn. You have no idea where you are and you pray that you will get a clue as to where you need to go. At that moment, someone honks at you because you are driving too slow or not paying attention to a light that just turned green in front of you. How embarrassing! I cannot count the number of times this has happened to me. I can see the locals shake their fists and shout, "Stupid tourist!" Quick, get my Google Maps.

The fact is, I am not stupid. I have a master's degree and did quite well academically. And I am a fast study at most things. It does not matter how smart you are, however, or how sincere and well-meaning, if you do not have the right information. You are just as likely to do the wrong thing as the right thing.

As I read through the pages of history, particularly the parts about the Christian religion, I just want to shake my fists and say, "Stupid tourists! What were you thinking? Did you not read the story? Did you not understand anything Jesus taught?" But then I remember "Tim the tourist." Sometimes I am more like them than I care to admit. Each of us only knows what we know. What we do not know, we don't even know that we do not know it. It truly is a blind spot. So how can I judge another person? How can I judge what they did or did not know?

Now, do not get me wrong. I am not making excuses for our dark times in history. Just because many people over the centuries did not actually grasp the meaning of God's wonderful story does not mean we justify the horrible things they did. It just means that I cannot be their judge. I have to leave that to God to sort out. Yet it's important to learn from history. So what can we learn from the story of the Christian religion?

First, we discover that the process of changing the human heart from the inside out is not a magical cure that happens overnight. God wants to change us, but Act Five reminds us that we have to be careful about losing sight of the key truths of Jesus' message, lest we drift away from God's desire for a radically loving community in the process.

Second, through the example of Jesus' early movement, we can find real encouragement. Even when the odds are stacked against us, even when faced by our own human frailty, it is possible for us to change the world if we embrace the revolution as the early church did. It is amazing what God can do with average, humble people. Paul's words to the Corinthians should give us hope: "But God chose the foolish things of the world to shame the wise; God chose the weak things of the world to shame the strong" (1 Corinthians 1:27).

Third, when we look honestly at the history of the Christian religion, we must confront the reality of how destructive religion can be. Religion as a system of salvation—a codification of ultimate truth that sets all the rules, defends the boundaries, establishes controlling leaders, and dishes out harsh punishment for those who do not get it right—becomes one of the most deadly influences on humanity.

Religion, whether it is political, like some forms of fundamentalist Christianity and Islam, or more philosophical, like some forms of Buddhism and Hinduism, has the power either to mobilize people toward violence (for its cause) or to paralyze people from embracing compassionate action in the face of suffering. But this is not about pointing fingers at all faiths. Certainly Jesus' call to abandon religion needs to be heard by all people, but first and foremost, it must be embraced by those of the Christian religion.

Fourth, we need to remember that we must live what we believe. Jesus taught that a "tree is recognized by its fruit" (Matthew 12:33). In other words, it does not matter what I call myself or say I believe in. It matters how I live it out. My life needs to be consistent with the teaching I profess to follow, no matter how imperfectly I live that out. It is not the label I choose to wear that matters, it is the outcomes of my life. Now, we do not have to go back into the history books and hand out pass or fail grades to all our spiritual ancestors. But we also do not have to deny all the horrible things that were done in Jesus' name. We can simply say, "Let the fruit on the tree speak for itself, but let me focus on how I will live today, now that I know the meaning of the story."

As I close the history books and turn my attention to the future, I am left wondering, "What might be the next chapter in this unfolding drama? And where is this all headed?"

11

Renewal

Act Six

THIS STORY IS far from over. There is a final and glorious sixth act. The curtain will rise one more time and this time it will not fall. In the pages of the ancient library called the Bible, we see glimpses of the future, particularly in the book of Revelation and a few select passages of Paul's writings. Woven throughout are hints of what is still to come, clues to the final, glorious act in God's story. [1]

Here is what we can piece together.

One day Jesus will appear again on center stage and announce that Act Five is over. Then he will come to rule and reign as the rightful King of all people. How is this new life described in the Bible?

It will be like:

a beautiful city descending from heaven,

a radiant bride just wed to her groom,

a joining of God and his people in an eternal covenant,

a land where lion lies down with lamb,

a world where all nations live together in harmony and peace,

a mountain from which a life-giving river gushes and flows into a beautiful valley where the trees of life line the river's banks.

Over and over again, the ancient books of the Bible paint joyful, hopeful images of the perfect world our hearts long for.

Even nature celebrates the renewal that Jesus will usher in. Animals, birds, fish, plants, the land, the sea, the sky, and the earth itself will be restored to wholeness and peace. The transformation leaves nothing untouched or unchanged.

But what of those who have died?

Jesus, the resurrected one, will raise all who have died so that they can join those who are still alive. He joyfully welcomes into his new creation all those who have humbly embraced his love, forgiveness, and life-changing power. Sadly, those who have willfully chosen to reject God's grace and mercy will be left out of the picture. They will face judgment, but not from a vindictive judge. They will be judged by the one who has the perfect intimate knowledge, wisdom, and grace to see clearly and judge justly. He alone will decide who is righteous and who is not. I am glad that is not my call.

The earth will be transformed, recapturing the vision of the Garden of Eden, but with one important difference: the tree of "I will decide for myself what is right and wrong" will not be there. Instead, God will plant many "trees of life" to nurture and sustain his people for all eternity. It is the beautiful, simple, and secure world God originally envisioned, now miraculously and completely realized.

However, from the abundant prophetic images of Revelation we see that something more emerges.

> Then I saw a new heaven and a new earth, for the old heaven and the old earth had disappeared. And the sea was also gone. And I saw the holy city, the new Jerusalem, coming down from God out of heaven like a bride beautifully dressed for her husband.
>
> I heard a loud shout from the throne, saying, "Look, God's home is now among his people! He will live with them, and they will be his people. God himself will be with them. He will wipe every tear from their eyes, and there will be no more death or sorrow or crying or pain. All these things are gone forever."...

> I saw no temple in the city, for the Lord God Almighty and the Lamb are its temple. And the city has no need of sun or moon, for the glory of God illuminates the city, and the Lamb is its light.
>
> REVELATION 21:1-4,22-23, NLT

In this vision of the future we see that there is no temple, no rite, and no ritual. Religion has disappeared forever in the new heaven and new earth. Finally, only love will guide humanity, which is being renewed into an ever-deepening experience of love, joy, and peace. Could it get any better than that?

There is no end to this drama. No curtain call. God embarks into eternity as the Divine Parent of one big, happy family, partnering together to make an already perfect world even better.

What will be the ultimate conclusion to my story?

What do I think awaits me at the end of my life?

Reflection on Renewal

It was my eleventh birthday, and I had nagged my dad so much that he finally took me to see *Star Wars*. As a junior-high boy who loved science fiction, I was spellbound. I remember the thrill of that final space battle as I sat on the edge of my seat. I remember the joy I experienced when Luke, Han, and Princess Leah were all ushered into the grand hall as triumphant heroes. I wanted to stand up and cheer.

As I mentioned at the beginning of our story, something in us longs for perfection. Decay, disease, death; we instinctively know this is not the way it was meant to be. As we gaze into the vision of God's plan to renew all things, we see the hope for all our longings. We see deliverance from all the violent spiritual and emotional intruders that we have let into our lives through our own rebellion. We see what a new community would look like. We see a light at the end of the tunnel.

In this final act, we are again welcomed to eat from the Tree of Life. Finally, we will not have to worry about getting old and dying one day. If you really think about it, we all have a sense that we were meant to live forever. We all know that death just does not feel right.

I have had many conversations with elderly friends who have said, "My body is eighty years old, but inside I feel like I'm thirty." When we are healthy and just living life we feel as if we could go on forever. When sickness comes or our body ages, it simply feels wrong. It gets in the way of living the way we want to. In the renewed world, however, we will be free just to live life, because aspects of our fallen world such as disease, decay, and death will be gone forever.

As I mentioned, there is something else that will not exist in the renewed world: the tree of "I will decide for myself what is right and wrong." In the first act, God offered the first man and woman the freedom to live in relationship with him or to walk away. This was represented by the choice found in the tree—to eat and disobey God or trust him and refrain from eating. Now, this raises a very interesting question: at the renewal of all things, does love not demand the same freedom?

I think a clue is found in the analogy of a wedding ceremony. This is one of the images God uses to describe the kind of relationship he wants with his people as they enter into this new phase of life together. The writer of the book of Revelation describes God and his people entering the renewed world as a groom and his beautiful bride.

Prior to getting married, two people share a love-based relationship that is rooted in free choice. If they do not love each other anymore, they end the relationship. As long as they both love each other, they stay together. However, if a person were to take someone hostage and demand to be loved, it would not be a marriage. It would be an abusive and illegal relationship, the act of a deranged criminal.

According to God's design, when two people decide to marry after an appropriate time of getting to know each other, their love for each other leads them to make a decision to give up their freedom to just walk away. They willingly enter into a lifelong commitment, and that settles it for all time. As they love each other equally and serve each other fully, this commitment is not bondage but freedom. It offers the freedom to love and be loved in a secure relationship.

As God's people, who once were free to walk away from God, we now realize we do not want anyone or anything else. Our commitment to him is for life, and in this commitment, like a bride committing to her groom forever, we enter into a covenant that secures our hearts for eternity. We do not lose freedom. We gain security, the security of a more mature and complete relationship, one that is rooted in a love that will never end.

There is one more thing that will not exist in the new world. All religion will be gone. We will not need a temple or priests. God finally gets us back where he wants us: living and loving together as a global family, celebrating the friendship he has wanted from day one. No more rules. Just love as our guide into an ever-deepening experience of joy and intimacy. Sounds amazing, yes?

This vision of a new world reminds me of C. S. Lewis's concluding statement in *The Chronicles of Narnia*: "All their life in this world and all their adventures in Narnia had only been the cover and the title page: now at last they were beginning Chapter One of the Great Story which no one on earth has read, which goes on forever, in which every chapter is better than the one before."[2]

Finally, we discover something both satisfying and sobering. Act Six reveals that every person who has ever lived will stand before God to receive what their lives have warranted. Though this event may seem like something to avoid or dread, it is actually something that should bring us a sense of closure. It is satisfying to know that God himself, with perfect understanding, fairness, and grace, will be the final judge.

Holding on to this conviction is important. It relieves us from taking matters into our own hands to seek revenge for wrongs, and it relieves us from despairing because people perpetrate evil and seem to get away with it. With the right view to the end of all things, we can simply focus on loving all people and living as peacemakers, resting in the confidence that God himself will one day right all wrongs.

This belief is sobering because it means that I cannot just do whatever I want, as if God does not care. He does care, and he has promised to settle all accounts. So often we are tempted to judge people harshly and demand immediate justice. When it comes to dealing with ourselves, however, we believe we are entitled to an endless number of excuses, justifications, and exceptions.

There is a great line in a song by Canadian musician Bruce Cockburn that goes "Everybody wants to see justice done on somebody else." That could not be truer.

My self-centeredness tells me that I deserve grace and everyone else deserves righteous wrath. But the knowledge that I too will stand before God means I need to wholeheartedly embrace the incredible grace God offers me. This is my chance to live, and I need to ask myself what I am going to do with it. What will be my values and priorities? What will I do with what I have been given?

The thought of facing God can become a source of fear that drives us back into our propensity to think that what God really wants is for us to become supersized religious fanatics. Remember, all God wants is our friendship. We simply need to trust and love. He has taken care of everything else.

In light of the great judgment to come, here are the key questions we should ask ourselves:

How can I best live out my life in partnership with God?

How can I weave my story into his story?

12

War

AS WE SIT back in our seats and reflect on the six acts of this story, there are some larger questions we need to address. Why did God decide to reveal his heart this way? Why would he reveal himself through Jesus and so humbly show us his sacrificial love? Certainly God could have come up with a different story line, one that would have spared all the struggle, pain, and suffering. He could have even spared his own suffering. What could be his motive?

In a few cryptic passages of the Bible we find a brief window into the larger spiritual realm, a realm of angels and fallen angels. Insights from these sections of the story reveal that our story is part of another, larger story. Here is what we can deduce about this from various Scriptures in the Bible.[1]

There was once a powerful angel—beautiful, wise, and in many ways an extraordinary created being. Somehow, he became proud and envious of God. He did not want to worship God. He wanted to be just like God. This led him to stage a rebellion—a kind of heavenly coup—that attracted one third of all angelic beings, who made war on heaven.

Ultimately, they lost their war and God cast them out of his presence and down to earth. Their rebellion and bitterness transformed them into enemy forces bent on the destruction of all that God holds dear.

> Then war broke out in heaven. Michael and his angels fought against the dragon, and the dragon and his angels fought back. But he was not strong enough, and they lost their place in heaven. The great dragon was hurled down — that ancient serpent called the devil, or Satan, who leads the whole world astray. He was hurled to the earth, and his angels with him.
>
> REVELATION 12:7-9

The chief fallen angel, fully corrupted through pride and self-centeredness, was the serpent in the Garden of Eden. He is called the dragon, Satan, the Devil, and the accuser. He is described as a dangerous, roaring lion pacing the earth in search of someone to devour and as one who masquerades as an angel of light, getting a foothold in our lives through deception in order to do his damage.[2]

Although we can only speculate on the details, it seems that the entire angelic order, both good and evil, forms the audience to the drama of God's story. Although those angels who rebelled knew the power and perfection of God, they never quite comprehended his love, compassion, and humility. Blinded by pride, those who rebelled thought that God was only about power and rank. They could not see God's true heart.

This part of the story reveals something that could never be revealed otherwise: God is rich in love and compassion. He delights in the humble but opposes the proud. He is the God who serves and pours out grace on the weak and broken. He shows us time and time again, most clearly in the life and death of his Son, Jesus, that ultimate achievement or success is not about attaining power and position but about serving and loving others.

By now God's heart should be clear to us. Religion, the idea that we can create and climb up our own stepladder of self-righteousness, stands completely opposed to the very heart of God. Not only do the rebellious angels who seek pride, position, and power get cast down, but so do all who try to raise themselves up to be like God in religious self-righteousness. Only those who allow God to change them from the inside out find friendship with him. Only those who abandon themselves to humility, love, and service find a lasting home in his presence.

And so, the most beautiful, wise, and powerful being in the universe next to God, full of pride and self-sufficiency, attempts to rise up and be like God. However, his desire to sit enthroned like God results in tragic consequences. In the end, it is not about beauty, success, power, or skill but about humility, service, compassion, and love.

After creating the angels, God creates a new kind of being. Not more powerful or beautiful or majestic than the angels. No, these beings are lower than the angels. God takes dust, just worthless dirt, and makes small, weak, frail beings called humans and gives them responsibility over all creation. But these new creations, made in the image of God, end up completely messing up. They are definitely on the opposite end of the spectrum from the angelic order.

So why did God make humans so incredibly weak and frail? The answer is revealed in the person of Jesus, who in his weakest moment dies a self-sacrificial death in order to rescue us weak, pitiful creatures. In his greatest weakness and humility, God triumphs over the power of Satan, sin, and death. Having opened the way for the complete restoration of humanity, God does the unimaginable. He decides to not only rescue the human race, but to adopt these same weak nobodies as his true children. Listen to how Paul expressed it in one of his letters:

> However, God is rich in mercy. He brought us to life with Christ while we were dead as a result of those things that we did wrong. He did this because of the great love that he has for us. You are saved by God's grace! And God raised us up and seated us in the heavens with Christ Jesus. God did this to show future generations the greatness of his grace by the goodness that God has shown us in Christ Jesus. (Ephesians 2:4-7, CEB)

Ironically, the seat of the power Satan sought to grab by force was freely given to us, the weakest and most messed-up creatures in all of creation.

In this way, we bring glory to God. Our weaknesses and failures reveal the magnitude of God's mercy and grace. It shows that to be God's friend you do not have to have impressive achievements or credentials. You simply have to trust him.

Reflection on War

I listened to my friend Jim describe an image he had seen in a picture. The three-dimensional sailboat in the scene sounded incredibly beautiful and detailed. I could not wait to take a look. When I finally looked at the picture, all I saw was a swirling design of color. He could obviously see something I could not.

Perhaps you have seen some of those computer-generated pictures containing optical illusions. If you stare into them long enough, an image appears. I am told the human brain has a way of assembling the various components of an image that at first seems unintelligible into something recognizable. They say that once your brain gets it, you can look at any of these "unintelligible" pictures and see the image hidden within the design.

In some ways this is similar to how we process the story of God. So much of it is counterintuitive; so much of it goes against the grain. Sometimes it is hard to get our minds and hearts around its truth.

For instance, I know I am not supposed to base my life on rules but on the love ethic of Jesus. But aren't some things just right and wrong, black and white? Jesus teaches me that I am supposed to love my enemies and not stay as far away from them as possible. But isn't getting close to my enemies dangerous for me and my loved ones?

I also know that I am supposed to treat everyone equally, even if their socioeconomic status is way above or below mine. But won't that lead to some uncomfortable situations? I am supposed to offer radical grace to people who mess up, not punish them. But what if they have done something really terrible?

There may be even harder pills to swallow. I am not supposed to hide my weaknesses and struggles or be embarrassed by them. Instead, I should embrace them because, through them, God gets the most credit from my life. Really? These expectations all sound a bit crazy. They go against pretty much everything we know as humans.

We are the masters at hiding our deficiencies, compensating for our weaknesses, and masquerading as people who have it all together. We have learned that if we do not cover up, we will suffer the consequences. We will not attract that gorgeous mate. We will not get that desirable promotion. We will not be accepted by the elite crowd. If we allow anyone to see our vulnerabilities, weakness, and failures, we set ourselves up to be laughed at, humiliated, and rejected.

One of the most striking things about the characters in the divine drama, however, is that God consistently works through people of obvious weakness. Not only that, God ensures that the biggest failures of people are written down for others to read for all time and eternity. Looked at in one way, the Bible represents one big book of failures. How would you like to have millions of people, century after century, read about your biggest mistakes and failures?

There is a method to God's madness. The book of Genesis describes our first parents as "naked and feeling no shame." As we learned, their vulnerability let them be completely intimate with each other and with God. They had nothing to hide because they were completely secure in divine love.

Today in our fallen, self-centered state we constantly hide our true selves, covering up our weaknesses and mistakes, hoping nobody will ever get to know the true "us." In this endless hiding and pretending, we find ourselves ultimately trapped and isolated from truly intimate relationships. We have to pretend we have it all together, to fake that we are fine. This leaves us all alone.

God's love offers us a wonderful solution. By embracing our frailty, failures, struggles, and mess-ups and then receiving God's grace, we can be free to be who we really are. All the things we want to hide about ourselves actually best show how wonderful God really is.

You see, your strengths, abilities, and accomplishments give the impression that you, in and of yourself, are a great person. If a successful business owner who appears to "have it all" wants to give God the credit, she or he has to stop people and say, "Now, I need to give God the credit, because without him I could not do it on my own." If they do not, people assume that the success is the result of how great a person he or she is.

On the other hand, when a drug addict who lives on the street, trapped in a destructive cycle of despair, is empowered by God to kick the habit, embrace a whole new life, and discover health and wholeness, people find it easier to say, "Wow! Obviously God did something pretty incredible in that guy's life." It is easy to see.

Even when someone endures real pain and suffering, opportunities arise to reveal how real God's grace is. Paul, the early Christ-follower, shares his own experience with this:

> To keep me from becoming proud, I was given a thorn in my flesh, a messenger from Satan to torment me and keep me from becoming proud. Three different times I begged the Lord to take it away. Each time he said, "My grace is all you need. My power works best in weakness." So now I am glad to boast about my weaknesses, so that the power of Christ can work through me. That's why I take pleasure in my weaknesses, and in the insults, hardships, persecutions, and troubles that I suffer for Christ. For when I am weak, then I am strong. (2 Corinthians 12:7-10, NLT)

This passage suggests that God used something really painful in Paul's life to keep him from becoming proud of his unique and powerful encounter with God. In fact, he is thankful for the weakness, knowing how easily human nature works in us to sabotage what God wants to do with us.

Once we humble ourselves and realize that we are not the stars of our own story, but rather look to find a supporting role within God's story, everything changes. The real struggles of our lives, then, no longer feel like failures. They become shining examples of how amazing God's love and grace are.

There is nothing left to hide. There is no longer any need to be ashamed of who God made you to be. The fact that you are weak, that you fail, and that you struggle to get through life the best you can, is exactly what qualifies you to radiate God's glory—not the glory of how great you are but the glory of his love, compassion, and humility.

I now have to look myself in the mirror and ask maybe the toughest question of all:

Is my life going to be all about me or all about God?

13

Improvise

DOES THE ANCIENT story of the Bible capture God's dream for humanity? Is God real, and could it be possible that this story is actually something more than the product of folklore and misguided mythmakers? Is this story true?

Some people believe in God. Some do not. Some look at the world and see a mechanical reality where natural forces explain all that exists. They just hope to live a good life before they die and decompose. I suppose for this kind of person the Bible is just an interesting footnote to history and means little else.

I have to be honest. I have tried to look for reasons why belief in God does not make sense, but I just cannot help but believe. I will admit there are some very smart atheists, and I respect their academic rigor. Yet I am left unmoved by their arguments.

Many of their arguments against the stories of the Bible are based on a failure to understand the actual meaning of the story. Remember, the church itself has lost touch with much of the meaning. Many atheists focus on the raw deal that religion brings to humanity—the violence, the legalism, the oppression, the hierarchical power system that tries to control people and influence governments. After reading this whole story, however, does it strike you as somewhat ironic that Jesus would wholeheartedly agree with the atheists on these points? Unfortunately, many people who have rejected God have only seen the confined, controlled, and joyless life that religion tries to sell instead of the abundant life Jesus promises to all who humble themselves and follow him.

With this said, I am led to believe in God for a reason more persuasive than any of the misguided arguments atheists sometimes make against it. I believe because I am captivated by the deep mine of truth I find within this story. Some parts of this truth may initially seem counterintuitive to me, but the longer I stare into it the more I am convinced it is right on.

I find the insights in the overarching story compelling. I see the architecture of a Creator in the beauty and order of the world. I see the incredible potential for both good and evil within humanity, and the story helps me understand why both are true. I understand completely that I cannot change my heart from the outside in. I need to be restored to my Creator and ask for his help to set my self-centered, fearful, and too-often angry heart right.

I am drawn to Jesus, both his teaching and example. That God would put an end to religion is a no-brainer. It makes complete sense to me that a Being of such intelligence, love, and desire for truth would want to transcend religion and instead seek true heart-to-heart friendship with us. I resonate with the vision of a global, inclusive family that prefers those who are weak and vulnerable. I am struck by the value Jesus places on women, children, minorities, and the marginalized. I am attracted by his call to serve others. I am challenged by his command to break the cycle of hate and love my enemies.

And then there is this idea of Jesus being "God with us." I know some people are intellectually offended by the idea of God entering into time and space to deliver a message to us personally, to break into the dysfunction of humanity and offer us a way to be friends with him one-on-one.

To me though, there is beauty in this. When my children were young, I would get down on the floor to play with them. I talk to them about stuff that interests them and use words they understand.

Why? I want to relate to them. I do not take them to work with me and try to get them to relate to me on my terms. As the mature one, I do the work of coming down to their level so that we can be fully connected and experience the amazing love between my heart and theirs. Does it not make sense that God would have the same parent's heart and, out of love, relate to us right where we are?

At the center of God's story is his own heart, which comes looking for us when we go astray and pushes aside every barrier that would stand in the way of close friendship with us. This most certainly includes bypassing all religion, possibly the biggest barrier ever created between God and humanity. God's love for us compels him to pay the highest price so that we might be restored to him, his lost children coming home.

Relating to my children helps me understand that kind of love. I will not let anything get between me and my kids feeling secure in my love for them. I will sacrifice whatever I need to in order to give them the best of me I have to offer. The divine drama tells us that God is no different. He loves us that much.

So this story leaves me asking questions such as:

Do I really grasp how valued I am and the value of those around me?

Do I view this world as an incredible expression of divine creativity and a gift to be treated with the utmost care?

Am I deciding for myself what is right and wrong and am I subtly trying to fix my life from the outside in?

Or . . .

Will I let God have the final say and just try to offer others what I desperately want myself, some kindness and grace?

And here are two big ones that hit close to home:

Do I actually want to be friends with God?

Do I want to know his heart for me and the vision he has for me?

For me, these two questions get at the core of who controls my life. *Who is top dog? Who is in charge?* You see, if I am honest, religion keeps God neatly packaged. God gets pressed into a bunch of rules, or is restricted to hanging out at the local temple, cathedral, or church. He is left waiting at the end of a long, winding path on which I try to work out my own enlightenment. Any way you slice it, religion ensures that God stays way out there and does not get too personally involved in my daily life or decisions. He does not actually have much of a say in anything, at least not the stuff that matters to me.

If he is my friend, however, and we hang out on a daily basis, if he connects with me and takes an active role in my life, then everything in it is up for grabs. He may have thoughts about what I do or do not do, what I own, what I give away, how I view other people. If I am honest, my first impulse is to think he could really screw up my life—in my mind at least, compared to the way I would run it. Yet, as I stare into this, I have to ask myself, do I really think I know better than God what is truly best for my life?

So, there you have it. I am faced with the choice. Is this my life, and do I want to live it all by myself without God? Or do I want to do life with him and find out what dreams he has for me? Jesus said, "I am the way and the truth and the life. No one comes to the Father except through me" (John 14:6). He could not have been clearer. He sidesteps all of our religious self-improvement programs and pathways to enlightenment. He puts it out there and leaves it with us.

What could it look like to be a part of God's story? For me, I think the word "improvise" describes it best.

This is what a typical day looks like for me. I start the day with just a bit of time getting my life focused on the right stuff. I view Jesus as both my director and my inspiration. As "God with us," I find myself drawn to him. I read something from the life of Jesus or other writings in the Bible and reflect on how that part of the story can help in my daily journey with God.

As I reflect, I quietly listen for something to resonate in my heart and mind. I ask, "God, what do you want me to understand about you and your approach to life that can guide me today?" I do not feel that he gives me line-by-line instructions about what to do and say in each situation but rather, as I focus on his teachings and life, taking time to reflect, I sense him encouraging and challenging me. I then begin to further reflect by asking myself questions like, "Am I expressing a gracious and gentle tone with people?" "Am I taking time to truly value others?" "Am I responding to others' needs or struggles in a practical way?"

I try to talk to God like I talk to a friend. Whatever is on my mind, I just put it out there. Jesus said we are to talk to God like he is our dad, and that seems simple enough.

I try to take time to see whether God impresses anything on me. It could be something I read or a sense that he is whispering a thought to me. I try to keep it simple and assume that if we are in a relationship together, if I ask him for something reasonable and if it fits with his overall purposes, he will help me with that request. By the same token, I determine to do the same for him. If he asks me to do something, then I try my best to make it happen just as anyone would in a loving relationship.

After that, I head into my day aware that God is constantly with me. I try to keep my eye out for where I see him at work in the lives of people around me. If I get into a stressful situation, I try to refocus on my connection with God to see what his thoughts are. I may need time alone to pray and think. I may need time with a trusted friend who can reflect to me God's heart and wisdom. Sometimes God does not give me the answer to a question, but often he provides perspective, and I get a sense of peace that everything will be all right.

The concept of family permeates this great story. God always tries to remind us that there are other cast members onstage sharing in this improvisation. They help me find the part I need to play in living out the story. The New Testament often refers to us as the "body of Christ" in order to remind us of our interdependence with other Christ-followers.

I am a part of a community called The Meeting House in Toronto, Canada. Its slogan is, "A church for people who aren't into church."

I guess you could say we are an irreligious church. Is that an oxymoron? Anyway, we use movie theatres, rented schools, and a converted warehouse as gathering places to hear weekly teaching and inspiration about Jesus and how to live as irreligious Christ-followers. We also get together in extended-family-sized groups in homes, where anywhere from ten to twenty-five people will discuss the teaching, ask tough questions, see how it applies to our lives, and challenge each other to action. We call these groups "home churches." For us, this is church at its best, where all our chairs face each other and we can support each other in our relationship with God.

As a church, we embrace the themes we see in God's story: pursuing peace, living simply, giving generously, sharing in community, and serving compassionately. We share a common commitment to invest significantly in compassionate initiatives, both locally and globally, particularly in the southern Africa HIV/AIDS crisis.

Do we do it perfectly? Probably not, but the heartbeat feels real. It is also a place where I can be honest with all my questions and hang-ups. It is a place that feels authentic, where I can be real, and where people can feel safe to ask hard questions and share the same heart. It is so much easier to live the story as a part of a supportive group that shares the same vision and approach to life.

So, in a lot of ways, my life may look ordinary to onlookers, but on the inside, I feel connected to God in my daily life. I feel secure even when I mess up, because I know I am deeply loved. I feel a clear sense of purpose. God's dream for humanity becomes very personal for me as God and I dream up goals for my life.

Even in the darkest seasons of my life, I feel God holding on to me and helping me. This world is messed up, no doubt. But when I get in touch with the core of who I am and take a look at the heart and mission of my church family, I feel like I am living the life God originally intended.

To do justice to this discussion about living this story, it really would take another whole study to examine what Jesus taught about following him on a daily basis and how he envisions a total inside-out transformation for us. There is also the question of how people can work together in a family-style community to experience this inside-out life change. So I will wrap up this book and start the next one.

Before I do, let's give Jesus the final word, it is his story, after all. When people encountered him personally and started to comprehend his vision for a new way of living, Jesus would quickly cut to the chase by making a very simple statement to them. He would say, "Follow me." He did not hand them a philosophical or theological treatise and say, "Read this." He did not describe a religious ritual and say, "Just do this." He did not dictate a strict code of conduct and say, "Obey this list of rules." He simply invited people to follow him. He was living the story, and he invited people to enter into the story with him. He was living the dream and welcomed people to make it a reality in their own lives.

It is so tempting to make ourselves the main character of our own autobiography instead of stepping into a greater story. Yet, if we take the risk, break free from the script we are trying to write, a new kind of adventure may unfold.

Maybe you are ready for a major plot twist in your life.

Imagine what may happen in your life if . . .

God enters, stage left.

Common Questions

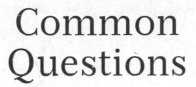

I WOULD LIKE to offer some simple answers to very common questions people ask about the story of God recorded in the Bible. Before I do this, though, a few disclaimers.

Many of the responses here are simple, abbreviated answers meant to give a few introductory thoughts. Of course, all of these questions would be better served with detailed, thorough responses, but I decided to provide a short-form version in the hope that these basic thoughts will point people in the right direction if they would like to explore these questions further.

Some people think that truth is plain and simple, and that if you cannot answer a question about God with a two-liner you are somehow blurring or misrepresenting the truth. This approach to God is not an accurate way to look at life. Consider the simple question of "Daddy, how is a baby made?" The question sounds simple enough, but let me tell you, to explain it fully takes more than a quick two-line response.

With that said, here are my brief answers to some common questions.

1. *Why do people not know the story of the Bible? Has it not been studied for centuries by some of the best scholars?*

First, the library we call the Bible is large, written in ancient languages, and rooted in cultural references that today are sometimes difficult to grasp. This library is not organized in a perfect chronological order, so it is easy to get lost in the story line, particularly regarding the story of Israel. There is a lot here to get your mind around. The phrase that comes to mind is, "You can't see the forest for all the trees."

Second, until the 1500s and the invention of the printing press, copies of the Bible were limited. For centuries people either did not have the story to read or the copy they had was not written in a language that was easy to understand. This meant that they relied on educated professional priests and pastors to dish out the truth, and so they often did not get the whole story.

Third, theologians have tended to dissect things scientifically and organize their findings systematically. That is like asking someone to describe me as a person and then have them tell you my height, weight, and the color of my hair but say nothing about my personality, passions, or life story. All the information might be correct, but that is not the way to get a full picture of me as a person. In the same way, theologians have often dissected the text of the Bible to describe God but have at times failed to communicate the meaning of the story.

Fourth, the meaning of the story goes against the grain of what people may want to hear. There may have been times when people have wanted to explain away the clear meaning of the story because they did not want to accept the potential implications or conclusions (for example, Jesus' command to love our enemies).

2. Does a person have to believe in a particular view of how the world was created to follow Jesus?

When it comes to the creation accounts in Scripture and the scientific study of evolution, Christians hold a wide spectrum of opinion and conviction. For instance, some argue for complete historicity of the first chapters of Genesis, while others maintain this passage is more of a figurative way to describe humanity's shared story. Some believe the conclusions around evolution are faulty or incomplete, and others accept them as accurate.

A person can be a fully committed Christ-follower and hold either position or be uncertain on the issue. There are many websites and excellent books that debate such issues.

3. *Doesn't God kill a lot of people in the Old Testament, like with the flood and the plagues of Egypt? How can he be a God of love and still kill people?*

Throughout Scripture, both Old and New Testaments, God is portrayed as the God of life and death. He alone holds divine privilege regarding all matters of judgment, life, and death. But it is important to keep in mind a few things about this.

First, God's perfection and holiness require that he not tolerate evil. This is a good thing, because if he tolerated evil it would mean that, at some level, he himself is evil, and then we would all be in a lot of trouble. What is really amazing, though, is not that he holds the power of life and death in his hands but that he is so incredibly loving and merciful.

Second, from the divine perspective physical death is not final death. God makes it clear that there is a final judgment after we die. Whatever the circumstance, whether by accident, disease, war, or natural disaster, all people will die one day and stand before God. We must weigh the bigger picture when considering what happens during our short time on earth.

Third, Scripture reveals that God has repeatedly rescued from judgment those whose hearts were soft and who tried their best to live righteously. Whether it was Noah and his family, or Lot's family, or other individuals, God preserved those whose hearts were set toward him.

Fourth, in Scripture we also see that when God's judgment falls, it comes on communities that practice terrible atrocities such as child and human sacrifice. Throughout history, humans have gone to war, killing and destroying each other in order to maintain a prosperous lifestyle for themselves or to uphold their honor. Is it right to criticize God for judging humanity harshly at times for the terrible abuses we have committed against each other? Think for a moment what men and women have done, and still do, to each other. Can we, then, honestly judge God for the times when he says "Enough!" and brings an end to our violence and evil?

4. *What about Israel's practice of animal sacrifice for the forgiveness of sins? Why did God want all those animals killed? Could God not just forgive people? Why did something have to die?*

We should first note that the notion of sacrifice is universal. Virtually all ancient civilizations practiced sacrifice. What was striking about Israel was that it did not include human sacrifice. This made them unique among their neighbors. According to the Torah, human sacrifice was strictly forbidden. But God did use animal sacrifice to visually reinforce the idea that sin leads ultimately to death.

Second, the picture of the innocent lamb shedding its blood for the people set the stage for the ultimate sacrifice for sins, the one paid by Jesus, the Lamb of God, through his death on the cross. This was a vivid picture of the seriousness of our condition and the complete forgiveness given to us. There was a practical side to this visual lesson as well. Some of the animals sacrificed in this system provided food for the priests, thus ensuring that those who preserved God's truth were provided for.

5. *Why did God give Israel such an involved list of laws, some of which seem harsh by today's standards?*

Neither ancient Israel nor the surrounding nations had a mature judicial system like we have in our Western world, with a police force, court systems, and prisons. The Torah, however, provided the laws the nation needed to survive, including corporal punishment for certain offences. When compared to those of neighboring nations, the laws of Israel would have stood out as incredibly gracious because of the ways they protected the rights of women, slaves, foreigners, and the poor, as well as their practice of regularly forgiving people's debts.

We must remember that the story of Israel is the story of what does not work. The Law, although given by God, was never intended to be a lasting solution for the human race. As we saw in the story, God clearly states that the Law would not work to change the human heart. Only in Jesus do we see a clear and full picture of God's love.

So the Law definitely falls far short of the love and grace we see in Jesus. Yet, as we look at the entire story, we can see that God had a purpose for giving the Law. It preserved the nation of Israel until the time God would reveal himself fully through Jesus.

6. There are a lot of crazy miracles in the Bible. Are they just myth or did they really happen? Is the story of Jesus not just a myth?

This question is like asking if a clockmaker has the right or ability to change the time on a clock he or she has made. The answer is, of course, yes they do. With that said, we should note that these miraculous stories are not common experiences throughout the narrative of the Bible. The people writing about them saw them as extraordinary.

We should also expect that as God intervenes in human history, he will at times effect things that will seem like a miracle to us. For instance, if I reach into a cage to change my pet hamster's water, from his perspective a crazy miracle just took place. Water appeared out of nowhere just because the hand-god appeared. Now I am not saying that we are like hamsters, but from our perspective, God entering our world and acting in power is really not that much different, is it?

In terms of the story of Jesus, virtually no serious scholar today disputes that Jesus was a historical figure. Numerous historical records, apart from the New Testament, support his existence and the rise of the first movement of Christ-followers. The broader scholarly community, both secular and Christian, accepts the core documents of the New Testament as first-century writings by the first Christ-followers.

As it relates to Jesus' life and miracles, the writers of these documents claimed that they were eyewitnesses (see Luke 1:1-3; John 21:24; 1 Corinthians 15:1-8; 2 Peter 1:16). Most importantly, they were eyewitnesses to the resurrection of Jesus (1 Corinthians 15:1-8 says there were over five hundred eyewitnesses). These first Christ-followers suffered severely for their beliefs, and many died for their conviction that what was later written about him was true and life-changing (see 2 Corinthians 11:22-28; Hebrews 11:35-29; Acts 7:54-59; 2 Corinthians 11:22-27). As we read and reflect on their accounts, we have to ask, "What convictions do I hold for which I would willingly suffer and die?"

7. If Jesus is God's Son, then did God not kill his own Son by making him die on the cross?

To better answer this question, we need to put it in the context of how God reveals himself in the Bible. God is in some ways beyond our comprehension, but Christians have formulated the picture of the God "Trinity," or the tri-unity of God, to help in comprehension.

Speaking of God as the Trinity means that our one God expresses himself in three primary ways: as God the Creator or Father, as the person of Jesus (as "God with us" or "God's word become flesh"), and as Spirit or divine presence that fills our lives.

Now, is God one? Yes. Do we understand him three different ways, as Father, Son, and Spirit? Yes. So are there three Gods or one God? We believe that there is one God but we know and experience him in three different ways. Some have used the illustration of water, ice, and vapor to understand God's nature. In order to connect with God fully, we need to embrace him as one God but encounter him through each of the ways he expresses himself. God is a relational but also transcendent being whom we do our best to understand through various analogies and metaphors. Now, every analogy breaks down when pushed too far. God is not an inanimate substance but fully personal and relational. Yet, the simple picture of the three states of water may help us see how something that is fundamentally the same substance can appear to us three different ways.

Consider also that God at his core is a relational being within himself. In a sense God communes with himself and can have a relational conversation between the various expressions of his being from our perspective.

It is the same for most people when they juggle many roles. Consider a man who is a husband, a father, and an employee. He may dialogue internally about how to best handle a situation as he looks at a single decision from various points of view. He may ask himself, "Should I quit working when it gets tough, or should I stick it out so that I can provide for my family?" If the only person he cared about was himself, then he may quit when things got too tough. Yet, because he loves his family, he will make sacrifices to ensure he cares for them.

When Jesus surrenders to his Father with the words "not my will but yours be done," he is expressing the relational nature of his internal being and exposes his heart to us so that we can see how much he loves us.

When we think about Jesus going to his death we should not think of it as God sending someone separate from himself to his death. Rather, we should think of it as God himself willingly offering up himself, a part of his personhood, for our sins. God did not die as a being, but taking the form of a man, Jesus, he experienced ultimate suffering, rejection, and death for us. This gets at the heart of this incredible mystery where God remains fully God and yet becomes one of us to experience life as we know it and to show us the full extent of his love for us.

8. *What does the Bible teach about Jesus as the only way for someone to have a relationship with God and to live forever in God's presence after they die?*

We know from Scripture that all people are equally loved by God and in need of a restored friendship with him. Based on the story of God from biblical teaching, there are only three possible responses to Jesus.

First, there are those who have heard God's story and have responded in faith to Jesus and are living in friendship with God. Scripture clearly affirms that these people will live with God for eternity after they die.

Second, there are those who hear God's story and the message of Jesus but choose to ignore or reject the message and follow another path. They may be agnostics, atheists, adherents to another world religion, or just plain uninterested. Scripture says that these people will be judged by how they have lived according to their own righteousness. We leave it up to God to make the final call on these people, which he will do in line with his infinite knowledge and love. But we cannot ignore that there are clear warnings in Scripture to people who hear the message of Jesus and reject him to follow their own path.[1] We have to be honest and say that according to the Bible there are no clear assurances for the afterlife given to those who do not embrace Jesus.

Third, there are those who may have not heard the message of Jesus or God's story at all. In this case there are indications in Scripture that God will judge them based on what they did know, rather than on what they did not know.[2] The Bible explains that God communicates in many ways and that deep down every human has a sense of what is right. Christ-followers trust that God will deal with every person in keeping with his mercy, justice, and infinite knowledge. There will be no technicalities or oversights on the final day.

From our limited perspective or sense of justice, there might be some surprises on judgment day. Some who think they have an "in" with God because of their religion will find out they never really knew God, while others who really do not know much about God will discover that, from his perspective, their hearts were in the right place. We see a hint of this in the story of a Roman centurion named Cornelius in Acts 10. He has no knowledge of Jesus but his heart is in the right place.

He is trying to worship God and serve others the best way he knows. It says in this passage that his worship was acceptable to God. And as soon as Cornelius has a chance to hear Jesus' message, from the apostle Peter, he immediately commits his life to following Jesus. With this said, we still see in the early portion of this story that his heart was already pointing in the right direction and God was honored by this.

Jesus himself indicates, in Matthew 25:31-46, that at the final judgment there will be many surprises. Some will think they are set up with God, but in fact they never knew God or understood his heart. Others will wonder why they are being welcomed into eternal life, when in this life they did not feel like they were living up to a full relationship with God.

Therefore, it is important that we not judge others or try to determine who is in the "in group" or the "out group." God is the final judge. That is his job, not ours. Instead, we should ask ourselves, "Am I in relationship with God? What is my response to Jesus and his call to follow him?" We cannot know what goes on in another person's heart. We cannot know how God will judge them. We can only account for our own lives and how we will respond to God's story and the message of Jesus.

9. *If the message of Jesus is about getting rid of the rules and simply following the love ethic of God, what about raising children? Are you saying we should raise kids this way? And should there be no laws, no police, and no prisons?*

Exchanging the rules, regulations, and rituals of religion for the love ethic of Jesus, we address the fundamental question, "What works to change the human heart?" We are not saying that these things have no place in society. Clear rules, strong leaders, and real consequences for bad behavior are necessary for managing external behavior. They can keep people from hurting themselves and others. They just cannot get us in touch with God, change our hearts, or renew our spirits.

As parents, we would be wise to teach young children with

thoughtful and appropriate rules, boundaries, and accountability, but as they grow older transition them toward the values Jesus teaches us as adults. The goal is not for children to know the rules to keep them out of fear but to learn to live in a loving, other-centered way. If they follow the latter they will know how to make wise choices when confronted with new or challenging situations. Their driving principle will be the love of God. The apostle Paul held the perspective that God gave the Law to the Israelites during the childhood phase of their spiritual development to prepare them for the coming of Jesus (see Galatians 3:21-25; 4:1-7).

10. *If the message of Jesus is that God does not want there to be any religion, does it mean that there is no value in rituals like Holy Communion or practices such as regular prayer?*

The early Christians did not outlaw practices associated with religion, but they always pointed to keeping their relationship with God as the key focus. Many early Jewish Christians continued to visit the temple and maintain practices such as circumcision, keeping the Sabbath, and maintaining dietary traditions. Gentile (non-Jewish) Christians by and large did not maintain these traditions but felt free to shape their own relationship to God without them.

The great thing about being irreligious is that you have freedom to shape your relationship with God according to your own personality. Some people love nature and connect with God just by going for a walk in the woods. Others love the beauty of art, music, and liturgy and connect with God as they experience these things. Others find that they best connect with God as they study the Bible and reflect on its teachings. Others still, enjoy quiet reflection and prayer and meet God that way. The key is to discover the best way you can live in close connection and friendship with God.

Bruxy Cavey, in his book *The End of Religion*, gives a helpful lesson about the difference between relationship and religion. He uses an illustration about a couple looking to spark romance in their marriage.[3] One couple might find that going out to dinner every Tuesday is a wonderful way to grow their relationship. Another couple might find that routine too boring and would rather do something different every week to keep things fresh. Rituals and traditions are great as long as the focus remains on the people in the relationship. If a tradition becomes a dead routine it can create the illusion of closeness when in fact there is no real heart connection, communication, or intimacy. Jesus frees us to put our relationship with God first and then within that love relationship to find an approach and rhythm that fits with who we are and how we best experience God.

The New Testament teaches that learning from Scripture, praying, sharing life together with other Christ-followers, serving others, and giving financially to the mission of Jesus are critical for all Christ-followers. Like all other healthy families, there are basic requirements for God's family, as all the family members learn, grow, and do life together. A committed Christ-follower's love for God and for people should be motivation to do these things with passion and consistency. Yet, each person must find their own approach to praying, learning, serving, and giving according to their personality and stage of life, much like different children in a family have different ways of contributing to the family or connecting with their parents. This is the freedom Jesus gives to all who follow him.

11. *If there are basically no rules and no top-down hierarchy, how can a church have leadership? How can there be any accountability and correction in community for people who are way out of line?*

The writings of the first Christ-followers make it clear that they viewed their gatherings as family get-togethers. They called each other brother and sister. Their leaders viewed themselves as spiritual parents seeking to cultivate a loving family. This vision of a spiritual family provides insight into how we can be an organized community with clear roles and responsibilities, yet maintain a high value for relationship and mutual submission.

A loving mother and father have leadership and authority in their family, but they use that authority to serve the needs of the children. And the children of a well-adjusted family will love their parents, honor them, and want to make their work as parents easy and enjoyable. Members of a healthy family may have disagreements, but they are committed to working their issues out together by respectfully listening to one another and seeking compromises that work for everyone. Children should have a voice in family decisions, but they also need to realize that parents still have to lead and make key decisions. There is accountability and correction, but it takes place within the family covenant and lifelong, loving relationships. This should be the model of the church.

The goal of a healthy family is to help each and every member become the best version of themselves that they can be. The same should hold true for the church. Most people realize that fear-based, dictatorial leadership does not work. It just makes everyone frustrated and good at sneaking the things they are not allowed to have. Loving, family-style relationships open up the way for people to work together to help each other, with clear leadership and a high level of commitment, support, and accountability.

The quality of family life rises and falls by what the parents and the older children do and what their attitudes are. Parents need to model what it means to love, listen, serve, compromise, and forgive. Those who are most mature must lead the way.

12. *How can Jesus be God's answer for the human race when the history of the Christian church has so much war, violence, and division?*

Just because people call themselves Christ-followers does not mean that they are. Jesus taught that you can recognize a tree by its fruit. Throughout even the darkest periods of the Christian religion, loving and gracious people lived the teachings of Jesus even when religious institutions were doing the opposite. Jesus said that those who follow him should not call him Lord unless they actually do what he says.

The testimony to the truth of Jesus is found in the lives of those who, over the centuries, have helped the poor, worked for justice, and offered grace to the broken. Although too often these women and men were an unseen minority, you will find them in every generation as you study the pages of history.

Even if we know the story, know what it means, the question is still, "Will we embrace God's story and then seek to weave our story into his story? Will we join his revolution and be an example of what a true Christ-follower looks like?"

13. *When you talk about final judgment, does the Bible not teach that there is a place called hell, where people suffer excruciating pain for eternity because they did not follow Jesus?*

For much of Christian history theologians have interpreted a number of passages in the New Testament to mean that there is an eternally existent place called hell, where people who have been judged by God will be sent to suffer forever as punishment. In recent centuries historical research has led a number of scholars to reinterpret these passages and reject the notion of an eternally existent place of suffering.

The most common word for hell in Jesus' teaching comes from the Greek word *Gehenna*, which was the name of a valley outside Jerusalem in the first century. Gehenna was the site of a public garbage dump. It had also been a place of idol worship and human sacrifice. To the Jews of Jesus' day, Gehenna represented the judgment of God. A number of scholars have therefore come to understand Jesus' teaching being not so much that if you are bad you will go to a fiery place called hell and burn for eternity, but more that if you live in a destructive way your life will go straight to the dump. In other words, the danger is not that you will go to hell after you die, if you continue in your bad ways, but that your life will be hell in the present (pardon the language).

So what do these scholars suggest will happen to those who are judged by God and have not believed in Jesus? Some suggest that their end will simply be death or nonexistence, much the same as atheists believe will happen after their deaths.[4] Others envision some form of redemptive path after death that leads everyone ultimately to a restored existence in a perfect world.[5] This may take the form of additional learning, a purging process, and a kind of holding pattern until their corruptions are purified.

So what is the right answer? Brilliant scholars have studied the texts and come up with different answers. Maybe the best approach is to keep it simple. Jesus challenges us to not wait until the other side to start thinking about where we stand on God and what Jesus accomplished for us. Jesus encourages us to consider that following him now is the best way to face death with security and confidence.

14. *How does God change the human heart? You have talked a lot about what does not work but have not said that much about what does work.*

This question provides the perfect segue to tell readers of this little book that I am working on as a sequel. My primary source is Ephesians, a letter written by Paul, the irreligious revolutionary, to people living in the city of Ephesus during the first century. This letter provides an excellent overview of how God changes the human heart. Here is a quick summary.

The key way God changes the human heart is through his presence. Once we are open to God, his Spirit enters our lives and provides a tangible, powerful experience of his divine perfect love. That love dispels our fear so that we can rest in the security that comes from our acceptance by God as his much-loved child. This is the first vital step in internalizing who we are as God's deeply loved children and close friends.

As we grow in the experience of God's limitless love, the community of God's family plays a significant role in renewing our minds, which is a necessary process in our spiritual growth. As the church unconditionally welcomes us, despite our flaws, it encourages, challenges, and teaches us. We then begin to internalize God's teaching and, with the help of our brothers and sisters, start the slow process of unlearning destructive mental and emotional habits.

As we learn to think in line with God's best for our lives, we then replace destructive behavioral habits with a loving, other-centered approach to relationships and life. This slow but steady process is an important aspect of what it means to be family, as we help each other, care for each other, and encourage one another to become the best versions of ourselves we can be.

I have much more to share about this from Ephesians and from my own experience, but that will have to do for now. The very best way to get going on this is to commit to Jesus as the leader of your life, and then ask God to start changing you as you get plugged into a Jesus-focused, Bible-teaching church family.

Bibliography

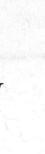

Chronological Bibles

LaGard, Smith F. *The Narrated Bible in Chronological Order*. Eugene, OR: Harvest House, 1984.

The Story: Read the Bible as One Seamless Story from Beginning to End. Grand Rapids, MI: Zondervan, 2005.

For people new to the story captured in the Bible

Anderson, Bernhard W. *The Unfolding Drama of the Bible*. Minneapolis, MN: Augsburg, 2006.

Boyd, Gregory A. *Repenting of Religion: Turning from Judgment to the Love of God*. Grand Rapids, MI: Baker, 2004.

Cavey, Bruxy. *The End of Religion: Encountering the Subversive Spirituality of Jesus*. Colorado Springs, CO: NavPress, 2007.

Fee, Gordon D. and Douglas Stuart. *How to Read the Bible for All Its Worth*, 2nd ed. Grand Rapids, MI: Zondervan, 1993.

Goheen, Michael and Craig Bartholomew. *The Drama of Scripture: Finding Our Place in the Biblical Story*. Grand Rapids, MI: Baker, 2004.

Wright, N. T. *The Original Jesus: The Life and Vision of a Revolutionary*. Grand Rapids, MI: Eerdmans, 1996.

Wright, N. T. *Simply Christian: Why Christianity Makes Sense*. New York: HarperCollins, 2006.

Notes

Chapter 1: Meaning

1. The most common term used for God's leadership was "Lord," which captured the sense of God having complete authority, ownership, and rule over a person's life.
2. I outline many of these reasons in my answer to the first question in the appendix Common Questions.

Chapter 2: Perfection

1. The author uses the masculine pronoun because no gender inclusive pronoun exists in the English language. God is characterized throughout Scripture as a person and being who possesses both masculine and feminine qualities. Rather than using the impersonal "it," the author follows the biblical pattern of using the masculine pronouns of "he," "him," and "his."
2. The ancient Egyptians believed in a huge number of gods and goddesses and that these deities could take animal form. They believed that Ra, the sun god, was the first god to touch solid ground. Ra created the god and goddess, Shu and Tefnut. These two got married and produced Nut, the sky goddess, and Geb, the earth god. Osiris was the god of the afterlife. These gods are the most significant in Egyptian religion. Between the major and

minor gods, the Egyptians worshipped over two thousand gods and goddesses.

3. William Sanford La Sor, David Allan Hubbard, and Fredric William Bush, *Old Testament Survey: The Message, Form and Background of the Old Testament* (Grand Rapids, MI: William B. Eerdmans, 1982), 73. Also see Walter Brueggemann, *Genesis* (Atlanta, GA: John Knox, 1982), 25.

4. John H. Walton, *NIV Application Commentary: Genesis* (Grand Rapids, MI: Zondervan, 2001), 130. Walton points out that in the ancient world people believed that an image carried the essence of that which it symbolized or represented.

5. Kenneth A. Matthews, *Genesis 1-11:26, The New American Commentary* (Nashville, TN: Broadman and Holman Publishers, 1996), 26, 52. Matthews points out the connection between the creation of the garden for the man and woman and the future Promised Land for Israel. In both cases we see the hope of a harmonious, fruitful coexistence of humanity and the created order.

6. Genesis 2:15 is often translated to suggest that God's command to Adam about the garden was to "tend it" or "watch over it." The Hebrew word used here is also the word to "guard" or "protect." This makes more sense in light of the unfolding drama, where Adam has apparently let down his guard and the serpent was allowed into the garden.

7. See Genesis 2:25. This passage sets the stage for the later confession of Adam in Genesis 3:10, "I heard you in the garden, and I was afraid because I was naked; so I hid."

8. Gordon J. Wehnam, *Word Biblical Commentary: Genesis 1–15* (Dallas, TX: Word, 1994). Wehnam provides an excellent overview of the scholarly discussion of this meaning of the Tree of Knowledge of Good and Evil and the decision to interpret "knowledge" in this case not as information about good and evil but rather as judgment over or mastery of good and evil, hence the translation: "I will decide for myself what is right and wrong."

Chapter 3: Broken

1. Victor P. Hamilton, *The Book of Genesis: Chapters 1–17* (Grand Rapids, MI: Eerdmans, 1990). Hamilton, as well as Wehman and Matthews, provides extensive material about the serpent and possible interpretations and understandings of the serpent's role in the narrative.

2. The "you" in Hebrew is plural, indicating both grammatically and from the flow of the text that the serpent was addressing both Adam and Eve at the same time, even though Eve is the first to respond and act.

3. Genesis 3:15. The statement to the serpent is "he [or the seed] will crush your head, and you will strike his heel." The verb "to strike" or "to crush" is identical in both phrases, but the impact of the action is radically different. The serpent receives the blow to the head; the seed receives the blow to the heel. The first is deadly; the second causes significant pain.

4. *The Matrix*, Warner Brothers, 1999.

Chapter 4: Struggle

1. See Genesis 4.

2. See Genesis 5–11.

3. In Genesis 8:20–9:17, God makes a covenant with Noah and future generations. This is the first time that a covenant is fully introduced in the story. See endnote 5 below for more on covenants. This covenant with Noah is initiated by God and includes new ground rules for all people. It includes God's promise not to flood the earth again, and the rainbow is his sign that he will keep the promise. In Genesis 8:21, God states that the problem with humanity is the heart's inclination toward doing what is wrong. This, we will see, is underscored again and again in the narrative.

4. There are numerous examples of this pattern in Genesis. These include Abraham and Lot (12–19), Sarah and Hagar (16; 21),

Isaac and Ishmael (16; 21–26), Jacob and Esau (25–36), Joseph and his brothers (37–50), and a scandalous example in Judah and Tamar (38).

5. The concept of covenant is important to the unfolding story of God. A covenant is a formalized agreement between two people rooted in love and loyalty. It is very serious and usually involves a lifelong commitment. God's first covenant is with Noah and his descendants (see Genesis 9). This is a general covenant for all of humanity. The second covenant is with Abraham, and it begins the process of God working through Abraham and his descendants to form the nation of Israel and to secure them in their own land. This was obviously significant for a nomadic people. This covenant with Abraham (see Genesis 12; 15–17) is restated for his son Isaac, his grandson Jacob (see Genesis 28), and his great-grandson Joseph (see Genesis 48). In this covenant with Abraham we see a number of key qualities. First, it was a covenant rooted in a trust-based relationship. The covenant with God did not require religious observance but rather faith, a complete trust in God. Also, the vision of this nation that would miraculously come from Abraham was that it would bless all the nations of the world. This covenant was God's starting point for the rescue mission he promised to Adam and Eve.

6. See Genesis 22.

7. See Genesis 25–36.

Chapter 5: Religion

1. In Deuteronomy 31:14-29, God clearly predicts that Israel will be unable to remain faithful to the covenant; they will break their relationship with God. God instructs Moses to write it down as a witness to the people. Both this passage and the prediction in the Law that Israel will demand a king (see Deuteronomy 17:14-20; 1 Samuel 8) clearly demonstrate that God was fully aware of the Law's inability to change the hearts of the people.

2. Exodus 1–12 is the story of Moses' call and the exodus of the Israelites out of Egypt.

3. In the biblical narrative, mountains, particularly Sinai and Horeb, are places where God meets with people. (There is a scholarly debate whether these are the same mountain or two different mountains.)

4. This is an important transition in the story of Israel. God resorts to a religious system with the nation of Israel in response to their lack of belief. Between the time of their liberation from Egypt (see Exodus 15) and the making of the covenant with them at Sinai (see Exodus 19–24), God allows the Israelites to march through the wilderness (a place of testing of hearts). This also took place with Moses and even with Jesus (see Matthew 4:1-11; Mark 1:12-13; Luke 4:1-13). During their three months of testing they consistently refused to trust God (see Exodus 16–18). When God leads them to Sinai to make covenant with them, they have shown they are not a people who trust God or can be trusted. So God is forced to deal with them in a way that uses Law to fence them in as his people for the sake of his unconditional promise to Abraham. This also explains the unusual choice of God in making a conditional covenant with them ("if you obey my word, then you'll be my people"; see Leviticus 26; Deuteronomy 30), rather than God's usual pattern of finding a tested and trusting covenant partner, such as Noah, Abraham, David, and Jesus, and then making an unconditional covenant with them. Paul in Galatians 3:23-25 describes the Law as a guardian put in charge over children to keep them safe, fencing them in and putting them in custody. The best religion can do is keep us in line. It can never change our hearts.

5. The Mosaic Covenant is outlined most clearly in Exodus 19–24 and is formalized with the nation in Deuteronomy 29–30. In a general sense, the entire covenant with Israel is captured in the Torah (the Law), the first five books of the Hebrew Scriptures.

Key elements of this covenant include the Ten Commandments (the Decalogue), the promise of Sabbath rest and the Promised Land, the priesthood, the tabernacle and the sacrificial system (ceremonial law), and the laws governing the nation (civil law).

6. Noah, Abraham, David, and Jesus all help establish unconditional covenants based on a tested and proven trusted relationship with God. It is only Moses' covenant that is conditional and rooted in a religious approach to God, with its rules, regulations, rituals, and routines.

7. For an excellent review of the Ten Commandments, see John Durham's *Word Biblical Commentary: Exodus* (Nashville, TN: Thomas Nelson, 1987). The original ten words were once listed as two sets of five and were easy to memorize that way. It begins with the title: "I am the Lord, your God." (1) "You must not have any gods before me"–"You must not murder"; (2) "You must not make any idols"–"You must not commit adultery"; (3) "You must not misuse the name of God"–"You must not steal"; (4) "Remember the Sabbath day"–"You must not bear false testimony"; (5) "Honor your father and mother"–"You must not covet." The final set of these commands does not refer to observable actions but to heart attitudes. Once paired and listed together it becomes easy to see the descending order of the commands, from most obvious and offensive violations of relationship to least obvious and internal.

8. One of the aspects of the Law of Moses that people often find offensive is the use of corporal and capital punishment. In this ancient period, there were no prisons and so the consequences of breaking the law were defined in very physical terms. What is striking in the Law are the provisions made to protect the innocent, women, slaves, and the poor. Again, when compared to today's laws (those that have been shaped by Christian values) the Law seems harsh and cruel. But when compared to other ancient civilizations it is incredibly merciful. For example, human

sacrifice and child sacrifice were widely practiced and this is strictly forbidden in the Law.

9. See Deuteronomy 31:14-22. Here God makes it explicit that neither the Law nor the Promised Land will ultimately make a difference for the Israelites, because their hearts are predisposed to wander. God shows mercy, however, by making provisions for a time when the people would ask for a king, even though he considers it rebellion against his own leadership (see Deuteronomy 17:14-20; 1 Samuel 8:6-9).

10. Moses' close friendship with God is explained in Exodus 33:7-11. Within the tabernacle was the Holy of Holies, which Israel's high priest could only enter once a year to make atonement for the sins of the people. Moses, on the other hand, could enter into God's presence and speak to God as "one speaks to a friend." Another powerful example of Moses' friendship with God is found in Numbers 12. Here Moses takes a non-Israelite wife, something forbidden in the Law. When confronted by Miriam and Aaron, it is these two who are corrected by God, not Moses. Why the special treatment for Moses? This account points out his humble heart and his close friendship with God. We should also mention that although Moses' close friendship with God transcended the Law at times, this close friendship also set a higher standard for Moses. Numbers 20:1-13 is a story of how Moses disregarded something God said to him directly. He broke trust with God and therefore was not allowed to enter the Promised Land. As God's friend, Moses was apparently not bound by many of the religious rules and rituals but rather was held accountable for what God asked of him personally. Beyond Moses, there are a number of men and women who received surprising mercy from God that apparently went way beyond the requirements of the Law and pointed toward an intimate friendship with God rooted in their humility and heart for God. Abraham, David, Elijah, Tamar, Rahab, Ruth, and Bathsheba are examples of this.

11. Compare Judges 17:6; 21:25 to Deuteronomy 12:8. Ruth is a scandalous contrast to this time in Israel's history. Ruth, a lowly Gentile woman, is one of the few people in Israel to actually understand what it means to live in a true trust-friendship with God. She will become an ancestor to King David and ultimately to the promised King, the Messiah.

Chapter 6: Kingdom

1. Old Testament scholar Walter Brueggemann argues that the temple constructed by Solomon represents ancient Israel adopting the religious framework of the nations around them. He demonstrates that Solomon's temple was, first and foremost, a Phoenician temple through and through. The second temple, referred to in Ezra, Nehemiah, and Haggai, was much smaller and less attractive, possibly closer to the tabernacle tent originally designed by God.

2. See 1 Kings 11:1-13. Solomon decided to marry influential foreign wives who served as royal signatures for international treaties as he formed alliances with other nations. His attempt to secure himself also included accumulating large amounts of silver (wealth) and horses (military hardware). In effect, he trusted in himself just like his tree-reaching ancestors Adam and Eve.

Chapter 7: Captivity

1. Often translated "Son of Man", this title is a common phrase in the biblical text that can mean an average person or a human descendant (see Ezekiel 2:1; Daniel 8:17). In Psalm 80:17, "son of man" is also used as a phrase to refer to Israel and portrays the "son of man" sitting at the right hand of God. This has led some scholars to suggest that the reference to "one like a son of man" in Daniel 7 may have originally been understood by the Israelites as referring to their unique role as a nation. This title, "Son of Man" or "The son of a human being", becomes Jesus' primary

title to refer to himself (for example, Matthew 12:40; Mark 2:10; Luke 9:22; John 3:14). The early church came to understand that Jesus fulfilled this prophecy and was this "Son of Man" (see Acts 7:56; Revelation 1:13; 14:14).

2. The word "holy" combines two primary images. First, it means to be set apart for a special purpose, particularly a purpose set out by God (see Leviticus 20:26). Second, it suggests being whole. The altars in the Old Testament were to be built with uncut stones so that the altar would be holy (see Deuteronomy 27:6; Exodus 20:24-25). Until the prophecy of Daniel 7, the phrase "Holy Ones" consistently referred to angelic messengers (see Deuteronomy 33:2; Job 5:1; Psalm 89:5,7; Daniel 4:17; Zechariah 14:5).

Chapter 8: Rescue

1. The writers of Jesus' biographies capture a long list of dramatic miracles, including command over nature, dramatic physical healings, raising people from the dead, and power over demonic forces.

2. John 10:30.

3. Matthew 28, Mark 16, Luke 24, and John 20–21 all record the resurrection appearances of Jesus, starting with the female disciples and then the other disciples. Paul in 1 Corinthians 15:3-8 records the most comprehensive list of those that saw the resurrected Jesus: "For what I received I passed on to you as of first importance: that Christ died for our sins according to the Scriptures, that he was buried, that he was raised on the third day according to the Scriptures, and that he appeared to Cephas [or Peter], and then to the Twelve. After that, he appeared to more than five hundred of the brothers and sisters at the same time, most of whom are still living, though some have fallen asleep. Then he appeared to James, then to all the apostles, and last of all he appeared to me also, as to one abnormally born."

4. See Luke 10:25-37 for a clear example.

5. See Matthew 5:43-47 and Luke 6:27-36 for clear examples.

6. Confucius in the sixth century BC was attributed with saying, "Hurt not others in ways that you would find hurtful."

7. See Mark 9:33-37 for a clear example.

8. See John 8:1-11 for a clear example.

9. See Romans 3:21-26; 5:12-21; Ephesians 2:11-21; Hebrews 9:11-10:18.

10. See Romans 3:21-26; Hebrews 9:11–10:18.

Chapter 9: Community

1. The early Christ-followers see Jesus after his resurrection and ascension as fulfilling the prophecy of Daniel 7. Jesus is consistently portrayed in the New Testament writings as being at the right hand of God the Father (see Luke 22:69; Acts 5:31; 7:55-56; Romans 8:34; Ephesians 1:20; Colossians 3:1; Hebrews 1:3, 12:2; 1 Peter 3:22).

2. See Acts 2 for a full description of this event and how their community celebrated together.

3. See Philippians 3:4-7 for how Paul described himself: "Indeed, if others have reason for confidence in their own efforts, I have even more! I was circumcised when I was eight days old. I am a pure-blooded citizen of Israel and a member of the tribe of Benjamin—a real Hebrew if there ever was one! I was a member of the Pharisees, who demand the strictest obedience to the Jewish law. I was so zealous that I harshly persecuted the church. And as for righteousness, I obeyed the law without fault. I once thought these things were valuable, but now I consider them worthless because of what Christ has done" (NLT).

4. "Holy Ones" is often translated as "saints" or "God's holy people." It is the most common name used in the New Testament writings for followers of Jesus (for example, Acts 9:13,32,41; 26:10; Romans 1:7; 8:27; 1 Corinthians 1:2; 2 Corinthians 1:1;

Ephesians 1:1; Philippians 1:1; Colossians 1:2; 1 Thessalonians 3:13; 2 Thessalonians 1:10; 1 Timothy 5:10; Philemon 1:5; Hebrews 6:10; Jude 1:3; Revelation 5:8).

Chapter 10: Christendom

1. During this period there are some amazing examples of people who lived in intimate friendship with God. Called the Christian mystics, they lived in intimate relationship with God. For a brief overview see Richard Foster's *Celebration of Discipline: The Path to Spiritual Growth* (San Francisco: Harper and Row, 1978).

Chapter 11: Renewal

1. Key Old Testament passages that foreshadow the New Testament teaching: Isaiah 65:17-25; Ezekiel 37:1-14; 47:1-12; Daniel 7:13-14. Key New Testament passages: John 14:1-4; 1 Corinthians 15:35-58; 1 Thessalonians 4:13–5:11; Revelation 21:1–22:5.
2. C. S. Lewis, *The Last Battle* (London: Collins, 1956), 172.

Chapter 12: War

1. Key Old Testament references: Genesis 3:1-15; Isaiah 14:12-17; Ezekiel 28:12-19. Key New Testament references: Matthew 4:1-11; 8:28-24; Mark 1:21-26; 5:1-20; Luke 4:1-13; 10:18; 11:14-26; 2 Corinthians 11:14; Ephesians 6:10-13; Colossians 2:13-15; 1 Peter 5:8; Revelation 12:1-17.
2. See Revelation 12:9-10; 1 Peter 5:8; 2 Corinthians 11:14; Ephesians 4:27.

Common Questions

1. John 3:36 is one of the clearest statements in this regard.
2. Many scholars point out that in Acts 10 Cornelius apparently had a heart set after God, even though he and his family had no understanding about Jesus or his message. When Cornelius

heard the message, he immediately responded. So scholars summarize that in the final judgment God may still save those who, like Cornelius, had a true heart for God yet had limited knowledge about God or Jesus.

3. See Bruxy Cavey, *The End of Religion* (Colorado Springs, CO: NavPress, 2007), page 51, "Blue Rose Tuesday", for an excellent explanation of this point.

4. One of the clearest descriptions of hell is Revelation 20:11-15: "Then I saw a great white throne and him who was seated on it. The earth and the heavens fled from his presence, and there was no place for them. And I saw the dead, great and small, standing before the throne, and books were opened. Another book was opened, which is the book of life. The dead were judged according to what they had done as recorded in the books. The sea gave up the dead that were in it, and death and Hades gave up the dead that were in them, and each person was judged according to what they had done. Then death and Hades were thrown into the lake of fire. The lake of fire is the second death. Anyone whose name was not found written in the book of life was thrown into the lake of fire." Here, hell is called the second death, which would suggest nonexistence for humans who have rejected God.

5. For an overview of understanding the different views about hell, see John F. Walvoord, Zachary J. Hayes, and Clark H. Pinnock, *Four Views of Hell* (Grand Rapids, MI: Zondervan, 1997).